Show and Sell...

Selling Your Home Today: A Cautionary Tale

Bill Hines

Wild Lake Press

Show and Sell: Selling Your Home Today

The author has taken care in the preparation of this book, but makes no express or implied warranty of any kind and assumes no responsibility for errors and omissions. No liability is assumed for incidental or consequential damages with or arising out of the use of the information or programs contained herein.

Copyright © 2016 Wild Lake Press

All rights reserved. No part of this book may be reproduced in any form by any means without the express permission of the author. This includes reprints, screen prints, excerpts, photocopying, recording, or any future means of reproducing text. The exception would be in the case of brief quotations embodied in the critical articles and reviews and pages where permission is specifically granted by the publisher (Wild Lake Press) or author (Bill Hines)."

First Edition, Version 1.0

ISBN: 0990907686

ISBN-13: 978-0990907688

LCCN: 2015918247

Wild Lake Press

Lake Hopatcong, NJ, USA

www.wildlakepress.com

Please send questions to info@wildlakepress.com and errors/corrections to errata@wildlakepress.com and include the book title and page.

To my brave and beautiful sister Donna; and my wife Lori, who stuck it out with me through all of the trials and tribulations described herein. —Bill Hines

Contents

Contents 1

Preface 5

1 Backstory, October 2012 11

2 To Realtor, or Not to Realtor? 17

    Traditional FSBO and MLS 17

    The Technology Effect 20

    Pros and Cons of Traditional MLS 23

    Today's Newer Alternatives 31

    Realtors are not 'Free' for Buyers 37

    Summary 42

3 The Price Is Right? 43

    Setting Your Home Price 43

    Pricing it Right the First Time 44

    Home Selling Competition 50

    Price Planning Strategies 53

    Summary 55

4 Prepping: Empty Nest Syndrome 57

    Getting the Home and Property Ready 57

    Pros and Cons of Empty Homes 58

2 Show and Sell: Selling Your Home Today

Preparing the Home for Visitors 63

Making Home Improvements 66

Home Warranties 67

Getting Pre-Inspections 68

Including Extras and Decluttering 70

Summary 71

5 Marketing: Putting It Out There 73

What is the Best Time of Year to List? 73

Putting Your Marketing Plan into Action .. 73

Picture Strategies 74

Keeping Things Neutral 77

Effective Signage 77

Creating Compelling Brochures 82

Using Business Cards 85

Social Marketing 88

Traditional Marketing—Newspapers 89

Preparing Your Website Pages 90

Other Marketing Options and Approaches 112

Summary 114

6 Show and Sell 117

Getting Ready to Show 117

Security Precautions 122

Handling Inquiries and Scammers.............124

Running an Open House 125

What to Expect When Visitors Arrive......129

Organizing and Giving Your Home Tour 131

Handling Private and Realtor Showings.135

Amazing but True Stories 137

How to Handle the Negatives......................146

Summary...151

7 End Game: Closing the Deal 153

Renting to Own and Other Options 153

Receiving and Handling Offers 158

Vetting the Buyers 161

Responding and Negotiating 166

Bidding Wars...168

Signing the Purchase Contract....................169

Moving Through the Process to Closing.170

Summary...185

8 Goodbye, and Good Luck! 187

4 Show and Sell: Selling Your Home Today

Appendix A: Chronology 203

Appendix B: Resources 209

Acknowledgement 211

About the Author 212

Preface

Like anyone else, when my wife and I needed to move, we had a lot of decisions to make. First, rent or sell our current home? Get a Realtor? Which Realtor? Sell or rent it ourselves? Make improvements? How much to sell or rent for? The list goes on and on. Moving is a long and stressful process, as are the associated tasks of finding a new place to live and relocating.

I dove right into the business of learning as much as I could about the current state of the realty industry. I'm a technologist, and therefore fully aware that traditional ways of doing things are being transformed by technology.

The beautiful thing is that these days, you can buy any number of inexpensive books on any topic, written by just about anyone. You can buy and download these titles for instant reading, and even preview free samples before making a decision to buy.

The bad thing is that a lot of them are not very good, or are written from a specific point of view. Most are written by Realtors, mortgage brokers, or real estate attorneys—not enough are by regular 'Joe Homeowners' like me.

6 Show and Sell: Selling Your Home Today

The books that have good content are often poorly written. Authors aren't motivated to pay someone to edit a book that brings in less than a buck a copy and will probably sell a few dozen.

Many of the books I read were rather dry and matter-of-fact. Some of these books were, shockingly, just a few pages. That's it? Oh well, those were less than a dollar. Who's to complain? The good news is that the open market has driven prices pretty low, so you can buy many books for what just one used to cost.

I read many of those books in short order. Even the worst of them provided me with more than enough value to justify what I had paid for them.

The best two books that I read were Sissy Lappin's *Simple and Sold* and *Home Selling Mastery* by Gary Marshall. I came across the book *Zillow Talk: The New Rules of Real Estate* after we were already though the process, and it had some helpful information that I'll reference in context throughout this book. (I provide links to those and other resources in Appendix B.) I carefully highlighted (electronically, of course) the important passages, and then copied all of my highlighted passages into a notebook app. The information was useful in every phase of our journey.

However, as we went along, we also discovered quite a bit on our own. A few things were specific to our situation; others were more generic, or related to the changing landscape of the real estate business.

In the past, home-owners have had two choices—go the traditional For Sale by Owner (FSBO) route, where no Realtors are involved, or the traditional listing/buying Multiple Listing Service (MLS) Realtor option. Put the emphasis on "traditional" in those cases. However, the world has changed, and continues to change, and that is the theme of this book.

In my research, I found that there is a newly emerging *middle ground* that has advantages for home buyers, home sellers, and (most) Realtors. It is really the best of all worlds, and a somewhat evolving revolution. This is the method we used, and which I'll describe in this book.

Toward the end of our long process, I felt that I had a lot to contribute on this topic that wasn't in any of the other books. I thought it would be fun to, well, have some fun with it—hence the subtitle...

A Cautionary Tale.

8 Show and Sell: Selling Your Home Today

We sure made a few mistakes and had some unplanned things happen.

I have attempted to make this more of a humorous tale, rather than a dry set of frightening facts and dire warnings. In telling our story, maybe you'll be entertained a little as you learn more about the process. I was shooting for a bit of tongue-in-cheek, a bit of read-it-and-weep. The good news is that no animals were harmed in the events that unfold here (just a few humans, due to psychological trauma).

This book is subtitled *A Cautionary Tale* for good reason, as you'll see. It may help you to realize that selling your home this way won't work for you. In that case, the book will also save you a great deal of time and expense. Realtors should love the book for that reason—it may be the best thing that's happened to your profession in a long time!

Some of the books I read were chock-full of links to resources such as home stagers and flat-fee MLS companies. I found that when I went to use those links, many of them didn't work, probably due to the companies going out of business. So I didn't want to clutter this book with that sort of thing.

I will mention and provide links to the service providers that worked for us. I feel it's only fair, since they did a good job and often went above and beyond the call of duty. I suggest you use Google (or your preferred Internet search engine) to find the most up-to-date information when you are ready to sell your house.

I hope you enjoy this book, and that you learn some things that will help you on your own home-selling quest. I've put some of the most important hints in easily identifiable side notes that you can skim through. Home buyers will also find tips in this book that can save them a great deal of money!

In any case, the couple of bucks you spend on this book could save you thousands of dollars or more. At the very least, maybe you'll get a few dollars' worth of entertainment value. Especially entertaining are the stories about open houses, where the people who attended did some of the weirdest and most disgusting things imaginable! I hope you will learn and laugh as you read this book.

Your reviews speak loudly, and I hope that if you get something out of this book, you can find time to post a positive review.

Bill Hines, September 7, 2015, at the Final Open House on the Lake

1 Backstory, October 2012

If this were a novel, starting with a backstory would be a bad thing, according to conventional wisdom. But, it's not a novel. All of you literary types can relax. Just enjoy the ride. Buckle up. It'll be a bit bumpy. Please place your seat backs and tray tables in the upright and locked position. Expect turbulence ahead. In this book, we're going to talk about how conventional wisdom can lead you down the wrong roads in today's real estate market.

I thought it important to fill you in on how we got to where we were, as it were, before this saga began. It may help to explain some of our later actions and the thought process we undertook.

It was a dark and stormy night (another bad way to start a novel). In fact, it was the night of Hurricane Sandy, which was in fact quite a dark and stormy night, and day. A month or so earlier, my wife and I had put in an offer to buy a great little place "down the shore," as we say in Jersey-speak. We were upset when someone beat us to the punch, and stole the place out from under us. We had always dreamed of living down the shore.

12 Show and Sell: Selling Your Home Today

On that dark and stormy night, as we watched the hurricane obliterate great sections of the shore (at least, until our cable went out), we began to second-guess the logic of investing in property there. We had both grown up in the same town and had gone to the same high school, a few years apart. We didn't know each other then—we met at a high school reunion some years later. Ah, but that's a love story for another time.

When we were kids, neither of us had been fortunate enough to live on the waterfront of our lake town. We envied our friends who did—those who had boats and docks and could swim and skate in their backyards. In response to my pleas, my dear father's favorite saying back then was "We don't need no boat, we got friends with boats." He was a wise and prudent man, indeed. That was not my opinion at the time.

Many years later, my wife and I decided that we wanted to finally have that experience. We began to think about living on the lake that we grew up near, rather than the ocean. We rented a waterfront home on the lake, with an option to purchase after six months, or allow the owner to put it up for sale. We learned quite a bit in those six months. Living on the lake was pretty cool. Living in a house high up above the lake, with a bazillion

Chapter 1: Backstory, October 2012

downhill steps to get there, and uphill on the way back, was not cool.

Living back in our hometown was not cool; unfortunately the place had a lot of problems. Shortly before we had to make our decision, the township jacked the property taxes way up, especially on lakefront owners, and devalued the properties to boot. Thanks, but no thanks! We informed the landlord that we did not intend to purchase, and started to search for a better lakefront home.

All of this contributed to our experience and knowledge, and would come in handy later as we bought and then subsequently sold our lakefront home. This backstory will help you understand some of the decisions we made and how our initial renting experience gave us some leverage and strategy.

Long story short (not short enough, you may be saying, under your breath) we searched for and found a lakefront home in a different township on the other side of the lake. We were able to get it for a good price because the couple who owned it split up in what seemed to be an acrimonious way.

This is the property that shall be the star of this book. Let's call it The House on Crazy Court. (This fictionalized version of the street name is not that far off and apparently named for good reason!) It was pricey, as lakefronts in NJ are wont to be, but my wife and I were both making good money, so what the hey. You only live once, as they say. (Actually, as of this writing, they say "YOLO".)

Oh, and guess that happened to that place down the shore that we loved and wanted so much? Yeah, Sandy wiped it from the face of the earth. We would have lost everything. A major bullet, dodged! Unfortunately, as you will see, the gun was still loaded.

Ok, still buckled up? Fast-forward to early 2015. We'd been in our new lakefront house about two years. My wife's job contract had ended, and she then found a fantastic new job (great news!), which was over a two-hour drive each way (not great news!). We tried and we tried to make it work. We didn't want to lose our waterfront paradise.

Also, around this time my company started a crusade to eliminate workers my age from the books and replace them with off-shore and on-shore H-1B-visa workers. It seemed that my days were numbered. Panic ensued. We were scared, with a mortgage and lots of dark clouds in our minds as we enjoyed our sunny lake home.

Chapter 1: Backstory, October 2012

There wasn't much to decide. My wife was valiantly attempting to commute without complaint, and keep the lake house. But I couldn't stand what it was doing to her. Okay, and what it was doing to the car. And to me.

We conferred with the Realtor who had sold us the house. She enthusiastically told us there was low inventory on the lake, and we should list our home for $70,000 over what we had paid for it. My wife and I looked at each other and we both had those giant dollar signs you see in the cartoon characters' eyes when they hit it big. Cue the music. Happy days are here again!

Not so fast. We still didn't want to lose the house. We kinda loved the joint. "Let's rent it out," we thought. "We'll let someone else make the mortgage payments. We'll let the property appreciate, and maybe retire to live there in the summer and somewhere warmer in the winter."

We wasted some time by listing it for rent with our Realtor. What followed was a ragged parade of would-be renters that consisted of dudes who wanted to share the house with like, lots of other dudes, to like, "party down" on the lake, and various and sundry other folks with either a circus full of pets, incredibly bad credit, or both.

16 Show and Sell: Selling Your Home Today

After that experience, we made the decision to put the place up for sale. We carefully read the rental contract, looking for any kind of penalty for bailing out. (Wrong time to do that, how about reading it before we signed it!) There wasn't one per se, but we did notice a clause stating that if someone bought the home while we were renting it, whether it was the one the Realtor found for us or not, that Realtor would be due a 6 percent commission.

That didn't seem fair at all, and we definitely wanted to get out of that situation. The contract stipulated that if anyone rented it within ninety days of us ending the contract, we still owed the agent. I guess that was to prevent someone from finding their own renter and trying to cut the agent out. Fair enough, but read those contracts carefully, people.

Anyway, by then spring was springing, and we figured, what better time to list a lakefront home for sale? So there we were.

Onward!

2 To Realtor, or Not to Realtor?

Our first decision was whether to use a Realtor or not. When we listed the home for rent, we had used the same Realtor who had originally worked with us when we bought the home. When we became discouraged with the quality of the applicants, we canceled the rental listing. We were focused on the big list price that the Realtor had recommended.

Warning—Don't Take the Bait!

Beware of Realtors that may give you an exaggerated idea of what your house may sell for. Some may do this just to get you to sign with them, and you and the home price will have to come down to earth after that.

Traditional FSBO and MLS

We began to consider the standard process of listing the house with a Realtor and getting it onto the MLS. One reason we questioned this, as you will see in more detail in the next chapter, was that we didn't have much equity built up. Paying 6 percent of our sale price to Realtors for commission would have taken all of our equity from us.

I had sold two of my previous homes myself, and remembered it being a lot of work, and the fact that they were not on the MLS was crippling.

Times have changed, as you'll see!

Many books advocate a straight FSBO model, shunning Realtors and the MLS. There are plenty of real estate aggregation websites out there today on which to advertise your home for sale, such as Zillow, Craigslist, Yahoo Real Estate, ForSalebyOwner.com, FSBO.com, and even eBay. (Trulia is another, but Zillow was bought by them in 2014, so we will refer to Zillow to represent both throughout this book.) None of these require MLS or Realtors. Homeowners can list their properties for sale on these sites, and some of the sites also pull information from MLS. They work great for the marketing phase of the process. But when you actually start getting offers, in the transactional phase, they don't do much for you.

Today and historically, the vast majority of homes that sell are listed on the MLS. That is changing, and doesn't really mean that the actual sale came from a Realtor. It may have been listed on MLS, but sold through direct contact between the buyer and seller using one of the sites I just mentioned, an open house visit, or private showing. A down-side of pure FSBO is that your property won't be on the MLS, and as such will not be visible to countless Realtors and their buyers.

Another big negative to FSBO is managing the transaction yourself, without a Realtor to guide you. You can download the legal forms from many websites to handle the transaction—let me know if they make enough sense to you to put your signature on them in a large financial deal. I doubt it, unless you are a realty attorney. This may also scare your prospective buyers away.

Warning—Legal Complexities

There are complex legalities in the process of transferring home ownership. It may be a very bad idea to try to navigate them without professional help.

A final negative to pure FSBO is that you will be hammered with phone calls, emails, and texts from Realtors who will be anxious to "help you" sell your home. I will discuss what I think is the optimum middle ground, and how to cover those problems and maximize your return throughout this book.

The Technology Effect

I'm a technologist, an IT guy. Even if you are not, you may have noticed that many jobs are being threatened by technology.

Taxi drivers are being driven out of business by Uber today, and will be by driverless cars tomorrow. Bed and Breakfast proprietors and motel owners are being replaced by everyday homeowners who rent their homes on Airbnb. Self-serve kiosks are showing up in restaurants like Chili's that allow you to view the menu, order and pay without a waiter or waitress. Even attorneys are being displaced by very good websites and software that allow you to put together a legal will and other documents for any state. Tax preparers are being replaced by software products that are better than they ever were. People are going to brick and mortar banks far less often than they used to, displacing bank tellers.

Technology is disruptive. So much today can be done entirely online, including document-signing and even 'face to face' meetings via video conference. Traditional middlemen in every aspect of life are being "Ubered-out" and those jobs are disappearing.

Years ago, I wrote two books and published them through a traditional publisher. I had to do it that way back then. The traditionalists had an iron grip on the publishing industry, just like Realtors and MLS used to have an iron grip on the real estate market. The parallels are strong in those two cases. Publishers would take your hard work, seize control of it, tie it up forever, and then perhaps someday actually publish it, and then take almost all of the profit. Now I self-publish. Today's technology provides fantastic tools that allow me to keep control, enlist the help of experts where I need it, and keep a larger share of the profits.

Realtors are seeing the impact of technology as well. Folks who decided to sell their property on their own would formerly (well, some still do...) stick the ubiquitous, ugly, red and white "For Sale By Owner" sign in their front yard and buy a terse ad in the newspaper. Now they can easily create a spectacular website on Zillow or Craigslist and reach potential buyers world-wide. You don't even have to know a lot about computers to do this. It requires no website design experience. You will see how we did this later in the book. Listing Realtors are being hurt by this to a large extent, and selling Realtors to a smaller extent.

Note that I said "listing Realtors." The real estate business is still operating under an outdated model where listing Realtors, the ones who list your home on the MLS, get an even split with the selling Realtors (or buyers' agents),who are the ones that bring buyers to look at your home.

Back in the old days before the Internet, when buyers had to paw through huge MLS books to find potential homes to visit, both listing and buyer Realtors did a lot of work. Both had to be present at home showings—but that too, was changed by technology. The lockbox was invented, and listing Realtors could just list the house and sit back while the buyer Realtors did all the work in schlepping their clients around from house to house. In some high-end markets such as Manhattan, both Realtors still show up. This is due to the properties being extremely high value, and sometimes difficulty placing a lockbox.

There are statistics that show that on average, a listing Realtor spends ten to fifty hours on the transaction, as opposed to buyers agents, who spend 100-300 hours. Most Realtors average just a handful of deals per year. Some realty agencies make the junior Realtors do all of the buyer-side hard work, while rewarding the more senior Realtors with listings.

Buyers' agents are being hurt by technology as well. In the old days, they held the keys to the kingdom, which was the list of properties for sale in their MLS. Home shoppers couldn't find homes for sale without asking a Realtor. Websites like Zillow have changed all of that.

You will see later in this book that by far most of the people that came to our open house or contacted us did so without a Realtor, despite the fact that we were on the MLS. They started their search in the comfort of their own homes, using attractive and powerful sites like Realtor.com, Zillow, and Trulia.

One visitor to our open house said "We just want to be able to look for a house without having to have a Realtor in the middle and have to work around their schedule to go and see properties, and we worry they might not be showing us everything."

Pros and Cons of Traditional MLS

We asked ourselves, what is listing the property with a Realtor the "traditional" way going to get us for the $14,000 or so in commission we will have to pay a listing agent? We made a list, as follows.

1. They will plant a big, obnoxious sign in our front yard. The sign will be a huge advertisement

24 Show and Sell: Selling Your Home Today

for the agency, and likely have a big picture of the Realtor, with little or no information about our house for passers-by.

2. They will probably put a terse description of the house on the MLS, such as ones we've seen similar to "NICE 3BR LKFRT!! 2BA!! CALL FOR APPT!!!" Don't laugh, look around and you'll see these for real. Someone is actually paying for that? Unfortunately, some Realtors don't have good computer skills and the aged MLS restricts how much space they have to enter content.

3. They would put an electronic lockbox on the door so that other Realtors (and only Realtors) can get in to show their clients.

4. They *might* have an open house at some point, but probably only one. What Realtor is going to sit at your house all day when they could be out selling or showing other houses?

5. They might feature our home in their Sunday newspaper ad, but even if that were to happen, it would be lost in a sea of many, many others. Do people really use the newspaper to look for homes these days? Not many, in our experience.

6. They may favor other properties over ours, not be objective, or be too busy to do a good job. The Realtor we were going to use to sell our

Chapter 2: To Realtor or Not to Realtor?

lakefront had a lakefront of her own that she was selling. I wonder which she drove traffic to first, and talked up the best? It's only human nature.

7. They would manage the process from showing, to offers, to inspections, to closing, pulling in the necessary finance people, lawyers, inspectors, appraisers, surveyors, etc. That's kind of a big job, and it all has to be done timely and in the right sequence. But will they be the best service providers for us, or simply ones that the Realtor or agency has some kind of relationship or agreement with?

8. Most importantly, they would put us on the MLS.

We tackled each of these point by point. I had used Build-A-Sign to create free signs for my Marine son's deployments and (thankfully) returns from Afghanistan. So kudos to this company and a shout-out here for doing that free for military families! I went on their site and saw some great home for sale sign templates. We'll discuss that more and show you ours in Chapter 5, "Marketing: Putting It Out There."

We lived in the house and loved the house for several years, so we knew that we could do a better job of writing a description of the home than some

Realtor who had been there probably all of fifteen minutes.

As we said, the MLS is still very antiquated and doesn't allow much space for descriptions, which is why Realtors use their forced, cryptic shorthand by habit and necessity. Some regional MLS sites have more capacity than others, so check to see what the ones in your area allow. The MLS descriptions are often 'fed' to other websites like Zillow that have much more capacity for text and pictures, but since it's automated, you get the same MLS shorthand everywhere! It really stands out, in a bad way, believe me. We didn't want that kind of description on our house.

Realtors will put a lockbox on the door and other Realtors will coordinate with them when they want to show someone the house. The Realtor will then coordinate with the homeowner, who may still live there. That's a lot of coordination and can be pretty frustrating to prospective buyers, which is what a lot of those who came to us without Realtors expressed.

We didn't want anyone frustrated, so we bought our own combination lockbox on Amazon, and achieved the same benefits without all of the middlemen. When Realtors called and wanted to show the house, we provided them with some great talking points, gave them the combination to the lockbox, and made sure we didn't have anyone else scheduled to go at the same time.

> **Tip—Cleanup after Realtors**
>
> *Always go through the property after realtors leave and before your next showing to make sure everything is restored to the way you like it, and to pick up the business card they will have left behind (save those).*

Realtors will leave a business card behind, and we kept those to follow up to see how their clients liked it, and to later inform them of any changes in price or other status.

We wanted to have a lot of open houses, not "maybe" one. Being on the lake, the house doesn't really *get* you until you are there, hearing the boats, feeling the breeze, taking in the scenery. Pictures don't give you that. We knew that we would be available to do the open houses, and heck, it's not such a bad place to spend a Sunday afternoon!

We didn't want the Realtor controlling our marketing. We know it's a business, and they can't afford to take the time and expense to take out a lot of ads. Every dollar they spend marketing the house is a dollar less for them, so it's understandable that they have to keep it to a minimum. We didn't want that. We wanted maximum.

An important factor was that our home was in a township that is desirable among the four that border that lake. One is considered by many to be an undesirable place to live based on the schools, taxes, infrastructure, and crime. People who live out of the area don't necessarily know that. A typical Realtor is trying to sell homes in all of those townships, especially to someone that has said they want to live on the lake. Are they going to tell a prospective buyer that Town A has these negatives and jeopardize a sale there? Heck no. They don't want to turn that buyer off because it's possible that the buyer doesn't know and might end up buying a house in that town, resulting in a nice commission check.

Are we going to stress those advantages to people who come to look at our house in desirable Town B? Heck yes! We are free to do that, the Realtor is not. We know the house, its history, and can answer any question on the spot with energy and enthusiasm. Some may say that visitors will be intimidated by meeting the home buyers, but in our

Chapter 2: To Realtor or Not to Realtor?

experience they were more intimidated by a Realtor, who is a professional sales person.

As far as item seven in our list, managing the process, that's kind of a big one, or it sounds like it. But really, who else is involved in the process? The buyer needs to get a mortgage, so a finance person is needed. Many buyers will use their own bank, or websites like bankrate.com to find the best deals. A real estate attorney is normally used on each side to manage all of the contracts, legalities, and closing. We decided we could make a handout for our buyers with some recommended resources on it. Besides, we knew that if the buyer came in with a Realtor, that Realtor would likely do the coordination, along with our attorney and the buyer's attorney.

Otherwise, there are service companies called 'transaction coordinators' who handle all of this for the buyer and seller, just as a Realtor would. One example is a company called Your-TC (www.your-tc.com). We did not use them, because as you will see we found a better alternative.

If you are reasonably organized, there are many websites that allow you to download a complete kit, or individual forms, for the entire process. I would not recommend trying to go through the process without at least an attorney review at every step, unless of course you are a real estate attorney.

Next, we discussed the MLS issue. That's a big one. While the MLS is in need of an update, it's still the conduit to the traditional real estate world and all of the Realtors out there with clients looking for homes.

Years ago, when I used Help-U-Sell and their do-it-yourself kit to sell my homes, the one major drawback was that you couldn't be on the MLS. Only a licensed real estate broker that is a member of the MLS can get you an MLS listing. Most Realtors, and MLS's, hold onto that for dear life and refuse to embrace the modern world. Big mistake! Keep in mind that MLS's are regional. There are many, many MLS's in the country, and probably more than one in your state. However, all MLS listings are aggregated to Realtor.com, and as such it is a truly national (and international) MLS website.

We wanted to be on the MLS, but didn't want to pay 3 percent commission just for that. By far, most homes are sold by buyers' agents, not the listing agents. So why reward someone with all that money just to put us on the MLS?

Chapter 2: To Realtor or Not to Realtor?

> **Warning—The Network Myth**
>
> *Listing agents will talk up their network and contacts as part of their sales pitch to get you to list with them. In reality, most depend completely on MLS listings and buyers coming to them.*

A good thing about the MLS is that by rule, the listings have to be unbranded and cannot tout or feature the listing agency, other than the brokerage name in the listing data. Mom and pop real estate agencies get equal billing with Remax and the other giants. And so do folks like us, who found a new way to get on MLS without paying a fortune!

Today's Newer Alternatives

In my reading, I discovered that there are now some progressive and smart Realtors who can see where things are going, and doing business in a different way. They know that the listing Realtor doesn't really do a whole lot to earn that fat 3 percent commission, and that's why home sellers are starting to avoid them. The real heroes/heroines are the buyer-side Realtors who are shuttling their crabby clients around from house to house every night and day. They earn their 3 percent share!

Progressive real estate agencies are now offering what are called "flat-fee listings." That's a deal where you pay a few hundred bucks ($400 in our case) and they put you on the local MLS and stand back and let you do your thing, if that's how you want it. Some, for an extra fee, will handle the coordination of the sale, broker any negotiations, and other services. They usually offer some number of a la carte services for the entire process from listing to closing, or do everything that a traditional listing Realtor would do, but for a *much* lower percentage of the sale.

TIP—You Don't Need a 3% Listing Realtor to Market and Sell Your Home

You can do almost everything a Realtor can do by yourself, plus a whole lot more, and dedicate your focus on your home, as opposed to the many homes a typical Realtor is juggling. All they typically do is provide you with an MLS listing, which you can get from a flat-fee Realtor and save a ton of money.

In weighing those factors, we decided to go the flat-fee route and do most of the work ourselves. We just couldn't face giving up such a huge chunk

Chapter 2: To Realtor or Not to Realtor?

of our return on the house to someone who we believed would do so little. I found many references to companies and websites that provided flat-fee listings. Some of them were already out of business (busted links), and I began to worry about where they were located and other factors.

Did they really know the local real estate law? Would they just turn around and farm out our listing to the lowest bidding Realtor, who would then try to up-sell us additional services or provide poor service when we need to do updates or changes? What if they went out of business? How responsive would they be when we wanted to make changes in our listing?

There is another myth that the listing Realtor should be local—based in the same area as the property that they are listing. They should know the local market conditions and have a sense of the buyer population and needs. If you are willing to do your own research, as I will show you, it isn't as important to have a local listing Realtor. Certainly the buyers' agents should be local, they are the ones that are showing and describing the house and surrounding area to their buyers.

Selling a home can be a very long process. Many Realtors who offer flat-fee will offer perks such as posting your ad on a variety of other websites, like Realtor.com, which is important. After they get your money, some will just find and work with a local agent in your area to get the house on the local MLS. Ask if they will farm it out to another broker agency or list it directly. Are they a realty agency or just a company that is farming things out to Realtors? Who will you work with to make changes in your listing?

As I said earlier, there can be many MLS's to deal with. In New Jersey we have Garden State MLS, New Jersey MLS, North Jersey MLS, and more. Realtors pay annual membership fees to each MLS they belong to. Realtor.com pulls data from regional MLS systems and consolidates it. If you talk to a flat-fee Realtor, ask which MLS systems they belong and will list your property on.

Warning—Regional MLS Systems

There are many regional MLS systems. Make sure you know which your home is going to be listed on.

We decided to take the safe route and find a real estate brokerage in our own state that offered flat-fee listings. After researching the choices, we found that Realmart Realty was just the right choice for us (they do handle listings nationwide). They were easy to work with, very responsive, and made our frequent changes immediately. Their CEO, Jack Yao, is a visionary who sees what is happening in the real estate market, and is passionate about this new way of selling homes. I'll relate more about how Realmart helped us in various chapters of this book. We have no connection with them, other than as a satisfied customer!

With this approach, you get your house listed without the typical 3 percent commission to the listing Realtor. You just pay one set "flat fee" and you are done on that side. Since this involves the MLS, you are required to pay some commission to the buyer-side Realtor. It would be wise to offer them the standard 3 percent, or close to it. You want them on your side and working for you. You don't *have* to offer the 3 percent commission, you can offer any percentage. But the lower you go, the less interest you will get from Realtors, and they are important. Some sellers that go the traditional route negotiate lower percentages anyway, so this is really no different. Offering a lower percentage may work better if your home is selling at a high-end price. In any case, 3 percent is a whole lot better than six.

As I said, those buyer-side Realtors are the heroes and work hard for that money. If a buyer comes to you on their own and is secure enough to handle everything without a Realtor, that's a bonus for you—zero commission. (Always check any flat-fee contracts that you sign to be sure.)

Realmart has an option to pay them 1 percent to do all of the things a standard listing Realtor would do, and more. They also have an option for buyers—if a buyer finds a home they want and hires Realmart to act as the buyer's agent, Realmart turns around and rebates them 2 percent of the 3 percent commission. Included in that are all of the things a buyer's agent would do, such as negotiations, organizing inspections, helping to line up financing, and closing. This is a great option for today's buyers, who want to be free to go to open houses and shop around on their own, and then bring in the experts to guide them through the transaction when they have found a home they want to put an offer on.

Some people would come to our open house, express interest in putting in an offer, and then say something about finding a Realtor to handle things for them. I always tried to talk to prospective buyers and explain to them that the Realtor's job is to find them a house. If they already found a house, they really don't need a Realtor—they need a good real estate attorney, perhaps a loan finance officer to help them find a good mortgage, and a few inspectors. All of those can be found like anything else—by using the Internet, checking ratings, and networking.

You have to be careful though. Some buyers will become suspicious that you are steering them away from a Realtor, and you may scare them away. This is particularly true of first-time homebuyers. It would be better to inform them of a deal such as the one I just described by Realmart, and what savvy buyer wouldn't jump at that?

Realtors are not 'Free' for Buyers

A Realtor will gladly step in at any point in the process, saying that their services are "free" to the buyer, but of course that's not exactly true. Somebody is going to have to pay that big commission, and that may appear to be the seller—but in most cases it's been added into the price, so the buyer is the one who is really paying it. If the seller knows there is a Realtor they have to pay, that will certainly hurt any negotiations over price. Some sellers even ask buyers to split commissions with them, and buyers may end up doing that if they've found the home of their dreams and it's a seller's market. So the buyer-side Realtor can end up not being free at all, on either side.

When we established our bottom price, we left some margin in case we had to pay a buyer's agent. We told prospective buyers that we had some room to negotiate—unless they were bringing in a Realtor and we would have to pay commission.

WARNING—Realtors Are Not 'Free' to Buyers!

Nothing is ever really free, is it? There is a fallacy that Realtor services are free to buyers. That's not true. If sellers know they don't have to pay a buyer's agent's commission, they most likely have more wiggle room in their price.

Some folks may decide to forego the MLS and sell on their own first, perhaps marketing through the usual websites that I talk about in this book. They may plan to avoid the MLS until they've taken a few months to try to sell strictly FSBO. It might seem to make sense if you aren't in a hurry. But there is still some stigma to 'For Sale By Owner' because of the bad old days, and once your house gets labeled as a FSBO in the hearts and minds of Realtors or prospective buyers, they may never notice that you listed it later on the MLS, or you may come off as desperate by doing so.

> **WARNING—FSBO Isolation**
>
> *You won't get much action from Realtors if you go pure FSBO, with no MLS and no offer to pay commission. When you advertise as FSBO, buyers or con artists may perceive that you are desperate and inexperienced and try to take advantage.*

We liked being able to tell folks that we were on the MLS, but doing our own marketing. This is especially useful to be able to beat back the hordes of Realtors who will want to represent you—they are prohibited to solicit any homeowner who is already listed.

Being on the MLS does give some level of legitimacy and assurance to nervous buyers. A home purchase is a big, big deal for most people. There may also be some negotiating advantage to buyers believing that you are paying a 6 percent commission. They will check the publicly available amount that you paid for your property against what you are selling it for, and try to determine from that what your bottom line might be. Zillow, for example, shows all of that information, although it isn't always totally accurate.

Always be sure to remind any inquiring buyer's agent that you are offering them a commission, if in fact you are. Some are still figuring out the new way of doing business, and quite threatened and confused by it.

I don't want to knock Realtors. It must be a tough job dealing with buyers and sellers, dealing with the stress of home buying/selling, doing all that driving, not getting a regular paycheck, and being at the mercy of the economy. It's got to be dangerous going into empty houses with people you don't know. Realtors bring a lot of knowledge and expertise to the table, especially those that have been "in the game" for a long time. I don't think they are going away, but are being transformed.

However, it's not rocket science, and in my crash course I think I learned enough, especially with the up to date information available on the Internet, to get this done primarily on my own.

As I've observed, the world is changing quickly. If your Realtor hasn't kept up with the times, you will be at a disadvantage against sellers and other Realtors who have. You may not want to deal with any of the work to sell your house

Chapter 2: To Realtor or Not to Realtor? 41

yourself, or may no longer be local enough to do it, and that's a good reason to use a full-service, traditional listing Realtor. But as we'll show, that doesn't mean you have to pay 3 percent on the listing side.

I would also say that you may not want to deal with the expense of buying things like brochures and signs yourself. However, if you figure that 3 percent listing commission on your asking price, that's a lot of expense right there, and you won't get much marketing for it—probably just an MLS listing. When marketing on your own, you will have to spend the money now, as opposed to paying the listing Realtor commission at closing. If the house doesn't sell, you don't pay the Realtor.

If you are more comfortable with a listing Realtor, and don't have the resources or availability to go it on your own, by all means use one. In that case I would definitely use technology to find one that has high ratings. Don't go by un-objective ratings like those on their own realty agency website. Zillow has real estate agent ratings on their site, and I would trust those. Other sites like Yelp and Google also show ratings for the Realtors and agencies.

Watch for tell-tale signs in your email communication with Realtors (they do use email, right?), as far as spelling, grammar, and communication skills. This is the person that will write your marketing copy! If the Realtor isn't savvy with newer ways of communicating, it will be frustrating for the younger buyers, who prefer texting over even email, and certainly over actual phone calls. If they don't have their own Realtor, they may reach out directly to your listing Realtor, who will be the contact on the MLS information that is pushed out to sites like Realtor.com, Homes.com, Zillow and Trulia.

Summary

I hope this chapter has helped you to make a decision on whether to go FSBO, flat-fee, or traditional listing/buying Realtor. No matter which route you have chosen, the next big step is to find the ideal price point for your house. We'll cover that in the next chapter, so let's move on!

3 The Price Is Right?

Setting Your Home Price

Now that the 'Realtor or Not to Realtor' decision is over, you can move on to the next big one. In our journey, by this point, we had found a rental and had already moved. My wife was enjoying a much shorter commute, but we were paying for both places, and wanted a quick sale. We reviewed the Realtor's enticing recommended listing price again. Remember, we later felt it was perhaps inflated in order to encourage us to list our home with her. But at this point, we hadn't considered that possibility. We were blinded by the possibility of selling at that price point, and making a profit.

So, we thought "Let's list it even lower, and not screw around." We listed it at $459,000, about $20,000 less than her recommended price. "This house will be gone before we can put the signs up!" we joyfully exclaimed as we danced around the living room arm in arm. I had received a list of 'comps' (comparable homes for sale or sold) from the Realtor as well as those I found on the major real estate pages (Zillow.com, Trulia.com, homes.yahoo.com, etc). I knew what I was doing, alrighty. Yeah, right.

We started doing more calculations. We had sunk a tidy sum into the place by renovating the bathroom (including a therapeutic Jacuzzi tub for the missus), among other repairs and improvements. Of course, we had also paid closing costs back when we bought it.

When we started to factor all of that in, plus a Realtor commission if the buyer came in with one, we realized that our small equity in the home would have been erased, especially if we had to come down in the price during negotiations. As I said earlier, this was a big factor in the reason to not use a traditional Realtor to list our home. What if the unthinkable happened and we got far less than we imagined?

Pricing it Right the First Time

Let's not get off on the wrong foot. Any seasoned Realtor will tell you, and the books I read stated very strongly that the thought process I just described is not the way to figure out your starting price.

It can't be what you *want* to get for the house. It can't be your "break even plus some profit" number. It must be based on what *that* particular

Chapter 3: The Price is Right? 45

property will sell for in *today's* market. You can best determine that by looking at all of the websites I've already mentioned for similar homes to yours, and what they've recently sold for.

Don't just look at homes for sale; look at the ones that have sold recently. The ones that haven't sold yet, especially if they've been on the market a while, may be priced too high, and therefore bad examples. While you are there, have a look at what the house was originally listed for and when it was listed, as well as how many price drops they had to do, and then what it ultimately sold for. If most of the homes have been sitting on the market a long time, you may want to consider waiting until things pick up before listing.

You can learn quite a bit about local and recent trends that way. Beware of anything that sold a long time ago and might reflect prior trends and economic circumstances. The rule of thumb is to use the last three months or so.

Some of these sites, like Zillow, will provide trending information on the zip code, township, and home itself. Learn about these other factors and take advantage of them.

For example, during the spring and summer we were selling our house, it was frequently in the news that the US Federal Reserve was going to stop propping up interest rates in the fall, which would result in higher mortgage rates. Even a small change in mortgage loan rates results in a big difference in how much someone pays for the home over a fifteen or thirty year loan, so we were not shy about mentioning that to our prospective buyers!

> **TIP—Price Your Property Right, From the Start**
>
> *They say you never get a second chance to make a first impression. Price your home correctly, as most of your attention will come in the first few weeks. Many may never look at it again.*

The guidance says that if you price the property right the first time, it should sell fairly quickly. That's just guidance, and not a promise, but it's critical to not come in too high. You will get a lot of attention and traffic in those first few weeks, and some might not come back after you and your asking price have come down to reality. A lot of things should be right—the price, the home's appearance (which we'll address in the next chapter), and your marketing materials (covered in Chapter 5). This chapter is about price, so let's continue that discussion.

Chapter 3: The Price is Right? 47

A big temptation in pricing the house high goes something like "What if some rich people come and will pay our inflated price?" Dream on! A big reason to not overprice your house is that even if you do find someone to pay the inflated price, a skilled appraiser for their mortgage company may not approve the price, and then you are back to square one.

The appraiser is going to do pretty much what I recommended that you do—compare the home to others in the area that are similar and have sold recently. If you have a lot of foreclosures in your area, it really hurts you since they generally sell well under value. If the buyers are paying cash, the appraisal won't be a problem, but most people use mortgages, especially when rates are low.

When I sold a previous house on my own, a buyer came in and offered us more than our asking price. I still haven't figured that one out, and was happy, until it was time to sweat out the appraisal. If you price the home at close to its true current worth in the market, there will likely be less haggling and emotion when you find someone who is interested. Remember, you have to find someone that actually likes the home first!

Another idea is to hire an appraiser yourself. There are associations that are reputable such as the American Institute of Real Estate Appraisers and the Society of Real Estate Appraisers. Check to see what it might cost to get an up-front mini or quickie appraisal (the type used for refinancing or home equity loans) and use that to set your price, and also to help your argument with any buyers who want to lowball their offer. In cases like ours, where the last appraisal was only a few years old, you may be able to get a 'refresher' appraisal from the same appraiser by showing them what has changed since the last one.

Another strategy is to list your home well *below* what you think it is worth. The thinking with this strategy is that you will immediately get multiple offers, and the resulting 'bidding war' will drive the final selling price up to what the home is worth, or even more. It's a risky strategy, but pays off well when it works. Remember, the property will get a lot of attention in those first few weeks after it's listed. What if you list it low, and then don't get offers? It's tough to raise your price when you aren't getting any offers. In that case, it probably means that your 'low' price was too high. What if you price it low, using this strategy, and you get *one* offer? Uh-oh!

The point is that every property has a certain worth. No matter which strategy you use, eventually, the home will 'find' its correct price and

Chapter 3: The Price is Right? 49

sell for that, like water always finding its own level. If you list it low, competing bids will drive it to its true value. If you list it high, you will get offers for its real worth (if you are lucky), or have to drop it down to its real worth in order to get offers. You might as well just price it right the first time.

We also agonized about the price in terms of should we go with something like $459,999, with all nines at the end, as is often recommended. To me, that always made the price look higher, no matter what the item is. After all, nine is the biggest digit in our decimal numbering system. I was also concerned about the house showing up when people search by limiting prices to something like $400,000 to $449,000. They don't usually use $449,999 as the upper limit, in my experience. That was also a factor in our early price drop from $459,000 to $449,000. We wanted to be under $450,000 in those searches. I liked the way the price looked with zeroes at the end, just cleaner and friendlier.

Later, when I read *Zillow Talk*, I saw their extensive analysis on this topic. I was happy to see their finding that recommends that the last non-zero digit end in nine, so we were good from that angle.

Home Selling Competition

You not only have to concern yourself with the appraisal of the home, but also remember that you are in competition against others who are selling their homes in your area. And believe me, it is a competition. Savvy home sellers and Realtors are in the habit of setting 'watch lists' by marking competing homes as 'favorites' on websites like Zillow. This allows them to get alerts when anyone else's price or site content changes. Don't get excited if you see that your listing has fifty followers—they might be mostly competitors, Realtors, and nosy neighbors/friends/family!

I noticed that when we dropped our price, the other lakefronts that were in competition with us followed suit. Use that competition to your favor. Look at each of those competing properties and their prices and ask yourself honestly if that home is a better deal than yours. It's very hard to be objective, especially about something we all grow so close to as our home. It's best to send the listings to other people that you can trust, and ask them to be honest.

> **TIP—Favorite Your Competition**
>
> *Compile a saved search using a few of the realty sites we've talked about here. It should include the parameters and area similar to your house. This allows you to get updates on anything that changes with your competition, so that you can react accordingly.*

Of course, the ones that have been on the market a long time may not be the best gauge—they probably haven't sold because they are over-priced. That's why it's always best to set the flag in your search that brings up properties that have recently sold when you are searching to determine your price. Those are the success stories and best barometer of what people will pay. Be analytic—this is a very important decision and it's a business decision, not an emotional one. And hey, if you don't have a lot of competition, you may even be able to sell above-market.

Factor in anything that the home and property need. People are generally very adverse to buying a home and then having to fix stuff. Most want to move in and start enjoying it (especially with the stress, work and expense of moving). Fixer-uppers and houses that are going to be 'flipped' (bought, fixed up, and resold) are exceptions.

We'll talk more about making improvements in the next chapter, but while we're on pricing, think about it. The one thing we were worried about with our home was that the furnace and central air conditioning were the original units, so they were old. We had them inspected and were told that they were working fine, but on borrowed time. We didn't want to replace working units, but knew buyers would be concerned, so we decided to include a home warranty to alleviate any concerns.

We advertised that prominently and mentioned it whenever the age of the system came up. A good rule of thumb is that the best improvements to make are fresh coats of paint and flooring.

We knew all of the things I've just discussed, but yet couldn't resist the temptation (driven by our 'expert' Realtor's advice) to list at what we wanted to sell for. We just couldn't come to terms with taking a loss on the home. After all, we've always been told that the American dream is home ownership. We've always been told that the way it works is that you buy a home and the home is an investment that you someday sell at a profit, because real estate always appreciates.

Unfortunately, that's not always the case these days. It seems to me that it's becoming quite rare. When I wrap up our story and this book, I'll give some of my own thoughts about how a home is now more like an asset that depreciates, like a car, and less like an investment, and why that has made me a much bigger fan of renting.

Price Planning Strategies

Time was a factor for us, since the home we were going to sell is a lakefront, and spring was upon us. We devised a plan where, should the unthinkable happen and our house not sell in the first week (insert sarcastic tone), we would drop the price systematically, ten thousand at the start of each month, until it sold. We figured that would allow for five price drops through September, in the worst possible case we could envision. So, we had a plan. It's always good to have a plan. What was that quote about the best laid plans of mice and men often going awry?

We set our opening price at $459,000. That would allow for a few price drops, expenses, and commission if the buyer came in with a Realtor, and still allow us to walk away semi-happy. We had bought the home for $405,000, plus paid the closing costs when we bought it, spent about $18,000 in improvements.

If we had to drop the price once or twice and negotiate down a little, at least we would make a little or break even and we could just look at those two and a half years of mortgage payments as 'rent.' There were unforeseen events in our future, as you will see. Things don't always go according to plan. Do they ever? As you will see, this strategy was a mistake. That's what this book is all about, so you can learn from our mistakes and experiences.

WARNING—Optimism is Your Enemy

Selling your home is typically a long and complex process. A lot can go wrong, and it's unlikely to go according to any plan. Always plan for and be ready for the worst case scenario.

The most important thing is to not list your home until everything is ready to go. The timing and sequence of the steps you will take are critical. If you jump out of the gate before then, you may squander valuable opportunities.

Summary

In the next few chapters, we'll walk you through the steps you'll need to follow in order to get ready and then pull the trigger to list at the most opportune time.

4 Prepping: Empty Nest Syndrome

Getting the Home and Property Ready

By this point, we had made our decision to sell without a traditional listing Realtor, to do flat-fee MLS, and the price at which we wanted to list the property. What's next?

There's always the temptation to put it out there in haste. The lingering feeling that people are out, looking at homes for sale, and nobody knows about yours. Your buyer is getting away! Resist the temptation. You have to be methodical and do it right. Mistakes can be very costly.

TIP—Don't Be Over Eager

Don't pull the trigger until everything is absolutely ready. Create a checklist from the things you learn in this and other books. Check and double check everything before you publish that first listing.

Pros and Cons of Empty Homes

We had already moved out, so the house was empty. That can be good and bad. An empty house certainly looks a lot bigger, but it looks, well, empty. No feng-shui going on here. There is a theory that the perception of roominess is what sells. An empty home also allows people to envision their own things in the different rooms, to see that there are no problems hidden by furniture, and that it's clean.

We had the home professionally cleaned after we moved out, and that was a great decision. A small army of little bitty women descended on the home like a swarm of bees and left everything bright and shiny after just a few hours. A good recommendation is to do a thorough vacuuming of the carpets if you have them, but save the money on a carpet cleaning, since you will (hopefully) have lots of foot traffic during your showings and open houses. However, if the carpet is stained or obviously dirty, you don't have much choice and may have to do a follow-up cleaning later.

If someone in the home is a smoker, or you have any kind of pet odor from cats or other animals, you absolutely have to remediate it. Don't trust your own sniffer—people who are used to it don't even notice. Find someone objective to come in and tell you. This is very important as so many people today have allergies to these sorts of things. Have it fixed professionally. It may involve repainting walls and a whole lot of Febreeze!

TIP—Use Professional Cleaners

Cleaning services are usually inexpensive and very thorough. It's a good idea to use them to get where you need to be in a hurry, for little investment. Save on the carpet shampooing, if it's not really bad.

We went back and forth as to whether the emptiness was good or bad. There are home staging companies that will come in and put in temporary furniture and decorate nicely. There are statistics that say staged homes sell faster than empty homes. Those statistics are often provided by the home staging companies. They charge a staging fee and rent you the furniture by the month.

There are also websites and videos for sale that show you how to stage your own home. In the end, we just couldn't get our head around the whole process of moving a houseful of furniture in, then out, and wondering what quality it would really be.

Heck, our home would be sold in days, so what a waste, right?

Our concern was that the empty room photos would look horrible on the websites. We didn't mind that the rooms were empty when people came to look. By then we had them there and could espouse the great features of the house, encourage them to visualize their own furniture, and it made the rooms look huge.

The first thing we did was dig out the old photos of the house from the online listings back when we bought it. I had downloaded those to my computer, so I still had them. You may also find yours around online, if you haven't owned your house long. Try doing a Google search for your address, and then click on the Images tab. It's amazing what's still out there! There is also an Internet 'time machine' site that can show you older versions of a lot of websites. It's called the Wayback Machine and it's part of the Internet Archive at https://archive.org/web/. (By the way, there's a ton of great music and other stuff on the Internet Archive.)

We got into a little trouble for using those old pictures, as we'll explain in the next chapter. The bottom line is that MLS does not allow you to post another Realtor's photos. We were asked to remove them immediately.

WARNING—Beware of Using Others' Photos

Be careful about using someone else's photos, especially a Realtor's. They may have been taken by a professional photographer and copyrighted. Always ask permission if you aren't sure. Lawsuits are no fun.

We did some investigation and chose a really great alternative—a company that does 'virtual staging' by taking photos of the empty room and inserting furniture into the picture. This includes pictures on the walls, drapes, knick-knacks, anything necessary to make it look great. The company we used was called Virtually Staging Properties (http://virtuallystagingproperties.com/) and they did a fantastic job with our pictures. It was far better than what we had hoped for, and inexpensive.

Figure 4-1 shows the master bedroom empty, and Figure 4-2 shows the staged photo. We didn't have to rent and lug any of that furniture up the stairs. We did this for several rooms.

Figure 4-1 Photo of the empty master bedroom.

Figure 4-2 Staged photo of the master bedroom.

Preparing the Home for Visitors

We did leave a few attractive decorations up. For example, a huge set of horns and a radiant bronze sun above the fireplace, and some things on either side of it to make it look nice. Remember, if you do this, the prospective buyer may well request those items as part of the contract. I was concerned about this, because the horns had been given to me by my late father.

We also realized pretty quickly that the house couldn't be completely empty. After bumping our heads a few times on the light fixture hanging from the dining room ceiling, we realized that it would also happen to folks touring the house.

We also wanted an area to sit and talk for a few minutes with our visitors, to display some brochures and other printed matter about the area and the lake, and perhaps put out some nice snacks. Oops, wish we had thought about that before we moved all of our furniture out! We moved in a glass table and some chairs that we had been using outside. It wasn't pretty, but it did the job, and after a while the lumps on our skulls started to go down.

We fixed up any marks and imperfections in the walls using some putty and paint, and those wonderful magic erasers. Imperfections like that stand out when the house is empty. Check to see if you have some remaining paint from when the walls were last painted. If not, taking a chip or sample to your local paint or hardware store will allow them to scan and match it with a fresh batch. If you have the empty can and the label isn't painted over, they can use that to make an exact match. Go through everything, including the basement and attic if you have them, and make sure it is all presentation ready.

Chapter 4: Prepping: Empty Nest Syndrome

Make sure there is bright, warm light in every area of the home. Buyers may bring their own high-powered flashlights to inspect areas of the house. Think about power washing the exterior. It really brightens up old siding, brick, or paint. Just be careful, power washers at the wrong setting can also remove any paint or coating.

In most cases, people are still living in the homes they are trying to sell. The same logic applies—reduce clutter, fix things up, take good photos. You may have to move some furniture or things out to take the pictures. Just remember that even if the pictures make it look nice, the clutter will look just as bad when you get people coming through to tour it. This might be a good time to downsize, have a yard sale, or put things in storage until your move is complete.

It's a good idea is to go through from room to room, top to bottom, and open every window, drawer, and door, checking for those that stick and may need to be adjusted, hinges lubed, or repaired. Make sure they all open and close properly. Use a careful eye to look for anything that looks out of sorts, such as nail holes in the walls that need to be fixed, or caulk that looks old or cracked. Make sure everything works as it's supposed to.

> **TIP—Make It Showroom Condition**
>
> *The house has to look fantastic both in your pictures and in real life when people come to visit. Not only to make it attractive to buyers, but as a reflection of what kind of people (you) they are getting into this with.*

Making Home Improvements

Most guidance says that you won't get close to a full return on home improvements, so be careful about making major investments just to sell your house. *Zillow Talk* has a very good, extensive chapter on this topic. Don't go putting a pool in. A lot of people don't want to deal with maintaining them, or the safety hazard. The two best things you can do, in general, are fresh paint and flooring. Beware of carpet—most of our buyers wanted hardwood floors and were constantly asking if there was plywood or wood flooring beneath the carpet.

As stated in the last chapter, if there are things that need to be fixed, you should fix them. If you don't, they will only be called out by the home inspector later, which will result in your buyer asking you to fix them, which could cause contention and delays when you least want them.

Be aware of and be honest about anything else, like we were about our aged furnace and central AC mentioned, and offer a remedy (the home warranty in our case). If you try to get around that "inspection contention" by stating that the home is being sold as-is, you will probably send prospective buyers running, wondering what else it is you are hiding.

> **TIP—Peace of Mind Sells**
>
> *Home warranties, pre-inspections, and having your old inspection documents on hand are a great way to ease any worries your buyers may have, and to get a jump on the competition.*

Home Warranties

A home warranty is a great thing to put out there right from the start. It's a bonus that may set your home apart from others on the market. It's something that is often negotiated into contracts by buyers anyway. They are about $400 for a year, depending on a number of factors.

Make sure to choose a reputable company if you go this route. We didn't actually take out the warranty up-front; we advertised that we would provide it as part of the sale. These are normally paid for at the closing, or the buyer is provided an allowance to buy their own.

Our intention was to allow the buyer to have some input as to what company we used (some have a bias from previous experience) and perhaps what options were covered. We also thought that some buyers would just rather have the cash to do it themselves, or well, to have the cash.

If your home has a good roof, new appliances, and a good furnace and central AC, there may not be a lot to cover and the warranty may not be a good idea. However, if there are new housing developments in your area, this could help if your buyers are weighing whether to buy a new or used home.

Getting Pre-Inspections

In keeping with the theme of making any prospective buyers feel comfortable, in addition to the home warranty offer you could get a termite and radon inspection in advance, and perhaps a pre-inspection of the whole home, as mentioned in the last chapter.

You can find a home inspector by going to the National Association of Home Inspectors web site

Chapter 4: Prepping: Empty Nest Syndrome

at http://www.nahi.org. If you have the inspection docs from having this done previously, or when you originally bought the house, have them available for anyone that asks. If these reports are recent enough, and you have a motivated and anxious buyer, it's possible that they might defer spending hundreds of dollars on their own inspection in lieu of these. That would save lots of time and hassle at closing.

In most cases though, buyers will want to do these inspections on their own, but providing peace of mind at this stage may well move them more easily into the next stage, which would be to put your home at the top of their list and make an offer. Not a lot of sellers do these things, so it can really make your home stand out by displaying confidence in it.

It would be good to know which walls are load-bearing and which can be removed. Buyers will come through with an eye toward making the place their own. Open concept floor plans are popular now, where there aren't walls between the kitchen, living room, and dining room areas. It's a social thing.

Including Extras and Decluttering

Keep in mind what extras you can include. In our case, since we were heading off to rent, we didn't need our fairly new appliances, so we included them with the house. It's attractive for folks that are coming out of rentals or relocating from a distance, or who want the property as a vacation, rental, or second home, or who may have old appliances in their current home.

We also had a nice 22-foot cabin cruiser sitting out at the dock. There would be no need for that after we sold our lakefront and became land-locked land lubbers. To make the package complete, we offered the boat, trailer, and accessories as an option to buy with the house. For anyone looking for 'serenity now', it was the complete package! We had the boat for sale under a separate listing on some of the Internet boating sites and Craigslist. At the bottom of the ad it said 'Comes with optional lakefront home for an extra $450,000." That got some laughs, but no home buyers.

Since we were renting somewhere else, we didn't need all of the homeowner accessories any more—things like our portable generator, lawn mower, kayak, patio heaters, power washer, outdoor furniture, and treadmill. I put those up for sale on Craigslist to make some cash and de-clutter the home. After all, the home would be sold soon. Right?

One benefit to doing this was that I got a few leads and lots of traffic to the house from folks who came to check out and buy that stuff. I made sure to give everyone a nice brochure to take with them to "show the spouse and think about how nice living on the lake would be."

Even if you don't live on a lake, you could hold yard sales to drive traffic to the home, hand out brochures, chat the place up, and maybe give some impromptu tours. "That coffee table sells for $20 today, and comes with an optional home, would you like a tour?"

Summary

The bottom line of this chapter is that the place has got to look great, inside and out. If you can, splurge for some professional landscaping. Just make sure you are using a very critical eye or ask others that you trust. Sculpting your shrubs into Disney characters may be ill-advised. It's likely that prospective buyers will be a lot pickier about what looks nice and what doesn't than you are.

Ok, got the house and property up to snuff? In the next chapter we'll talk about how to get your marketing materials ready.

5 Marketing: Putting It Out There

What is the Best Time of Year to List?

The "conventional wisdom" says that you want to list your house when the weather is comfortable for buyers to do their home shopping. The book *Zillow Talk* has a great deal of information on this topic. If you must list during cold-weather months, a study by online brokerage Redfin found that sellers sold more quickly and got better prices for their properties in those months. That may be due to buyers who must buy during those months being in more of a hurry, due to relocation and similar circumstances.

Putting Your Marketing Plan into Action

When the house is physically ready, it's time to put your marketing plan into action—or, if you don't have one, to build it. Measure twice, cut once! We'll talk about a number of marketing approaches in this chapter. They range from very popular websites like Zillow, Craigslist, and Yahoo Real Estate that allow you to create a nice web page for free, to a few more eclectic approaches that we came up with. I recommend that you do things in the order I prescribe for the fewest unpleasant surprises and least amount of hassle.

Picture Strategies

Start with good pictures. Really good pictures! I talked about this in the last chapter, but it's pertinent here as well, since those pictures are going to be your draw in today's multimedia Internet-based world. If your home is empty, I recommend getting staged photos done. As discussed in the last chapter, we used Virtually Staging Properties for ours. See the result of their work in Figures 4-1 and 4-2.

If your home is not vacant, de-clutter the rooms, walls, counters, and shelves. I was shocked at some of the horrible pictures that some of our competing homes had on their websites.

In the old days (well, even today for many MLS's) you could only have one or a couple of photos with your listing. In today's world, sites like Zillow and Craigslist allow you to put many photos

Chapter 5: Marketing: Putting It Out There

on your page. Don't overdo it though, or people may get overwhelmed and lose interest.

Organize your photos on those pages as if you are taking the viewer on a tour. Show the outside first, and then move inside from room to room. Random photos are confusing.

Chose the best picture as your main photo. That's the one you want to catch the viewer's eye. Many sites allow you to insert captions for the photos—take advantage of this. Don't use boring captions like "Living room." Talk about the unique features of each room in vibrant language that will get your prospective buyer anxious to come and see it in person. Make sure your spelling and grammar are correct.

TIP—Photos Are Very Important

We're a visual species, even more now than ever. People don't want to read. They want to look at pretty pictures. Put a lot into your photos, they will drive traffic. Take the time to put imaginative captions with the photos, and organize them so that they flow room to room.

Another factor to consider is the size of the pictures. You may think it's best to set your camera at the highest resolution, because you want the sharpest picture. That's not a bad idea, except that some websites have limitations on the size of images that can be uploaded. So you either have to compromise to meet the lowest common denominator, or learn to use picture editing software to take a hi-res photo and create a lower-res version of it for those sites. Or, better yet, enlist the help of a friend or relative who understand such things.

It's really not that hard to modify the picture resolution using software. If you have a computer that runs Microsoft Windows, it should have an application called Paint that has a 'Resize' choice in the menu. I used Adobe Photoshop Elements, which was fairly inexpensive at Costco. You may have to play around with your software to get the hang of it. Sometimes the pictures may look huge or tiny, but they can always be stretched to size no matter what their resolution. Most of the realty websites do a great job of stretching them optimally for display on their pages.

Keeping Things Neutral

Avoid showing anything in your pictures that might turn people off for religious, political, or other reasons. Some New York Giants fans I know wouldn't buy a house from anyone that is a Dallas Cowboys fan. At best, it could lead to testy conflicts during the stressful process of negotiating and closing. This applies when you are showing the home as well, of course. We'll talk about that in the next chapter.

WARNING—Disturbing Content
Keep the photos and home as neutral as possible in terms of religious, political, or sports team points of view. Remove your family pictures so that they can more easily visualize it as 'their' home.

Effective Signage

When preparing the property for your showings, tackle the things that are time-consuming first. For example, you will want a very nice yard sign, or maybe a few of them. We had one in the front of our house, and one out on our dock facing the boat traffic on the lake. We also ordered some less expensive signs to put up at strategic corners around the area to point people to our open houses.

As I said in Chapter 2, the company that we used (and I will absolutely endorse) is Build-A-Sign (http://www.buildasign.com/). They have excellent customer service, great prices, fantastic tools for designing signs, templates to get you started, and they provide free signs for our military veterans who are returning home or going away.

Figure 5-1 shows the aluminum sign that we designed. (I changed the phone number, of course.) I think you will agree, it looks a lot better than the typical real estate advertisement sign that Realtors will plop in your lawn. The print version of this book shows it in black and white—for the full color effect of this and other images see the electronic version of this book. Note that it doesn't say "For Sale by Owner" because of the stigmas that I discussed earlier in the book. However, we were quick to introduce ourselves as the owners to anyone that enquired.

This sign sat proudly in front of our home for the entire six months in the pouring rain and blazing sun, and never lost its color or sheen. Our brochure box hung from the steel frame that we bought with the sign. We often saw people drive up, inspect the sign, point at features, have a

Chapter 5: Marketing: Putting It Out There

discussion between themselves, and then take a brochure.

FOR SALE
Fish, Swim, Boat in your own backyard!
3BR, 2BA, 1 yr warranty. Take a brochure!

Two Fireplaces
Under-home Storage
Bill Hines
555-555-5555

Figure 5-1 Home for sale yard sign.

We had three directional signs to advertise our open house days and point folks in the right direction when they were trying to find the house. We came up with that number just by looking at the area and thinking about the most strategic places to put them. Figure 5-2 shows one of our directional signs.

You might think they are unnecessary, since most people use GPS to get around today. For us, it was a very good investment—in fact many people commented to us that they hadn't set out that day to look at homes, but had just been in the area, enjoying the lake, and saw the open house signs and decided to drop by. You never know.

Figure 5-2 Directional signs.

TIP—Tax Deductions

Certain home selling costs, such as repairs, staging, and advertising are be tax deductible, with a few caveats. Keep all of your receipts together and check with your tax accountant.

Chapter 5: Marketing: Putting It Out There

The signs on your property should have some form of 'brochure box' attached to them. It should be waterproof. We bought one on Amazon for just a few bucks, it was clear plastic and it did the job very well, despite being constantly pounded by rain and the lawn sprinkler. Put the sign and brochure box out at the front of the property by the road. Many folks are too shy to come up to the house (or afraid, or in too much of a hurry to get out of the car).

Usually, these products say 'Take One' on the outside. We had one out front, and another attached to our dock to attract boat traffic from the lake.

TIP—Signage and Brochures

A quality sign says a lot about you as homeowners and people, and makes people more at ease than the ubiquitous, ugly red and white "FSBO" sign. Always make sure you have brochures handy—we went through dozens and dozens.

You may wonder how we knew when the brochure box was empty. We had security cameras at the house, and those were a great way to monitor the situation, especially since we had a clear brochure box. If we could see the street through it, it was empty! If you have neighbors that can keep an eye for you, if your house is vacant like ours was, that's another good way.

We were making regular trips to the house to maintain the property and for our open houses, so we used those as opportunities to restock. Definitely don't run out of brochures. Many people don't want to take the time for a tour until they know a lot of specifics about the home. Our brochures had all of that

Creating Compelling Brochures

We created a tri-fold brochure that folded to show the most important details, with one picture on the front. There was a lot more information on the inside, and the entire back was filled with pictures. If you design and print brochures yourself, it's not that expensive. Remember the thousands of dollars you are saving in Realtor commissions.

Be very careful about including details that can change. Once that happens, you'll have to toss your inventory of brochures or use messy alternatives like white-out. However, omitting the price will frustrate your potential buyers. We learned to print only a few dozen at a time. Since color printer ink is expensive, it may be less expensive to print these at your local office supply store or printing business. We used Staples because we have a corporate discount, and we usually needed things from there anyway.

Figure 5-3 shows the back of our brochure (which became the front when we tri-folded it). The other side was filled with full-color pictures.

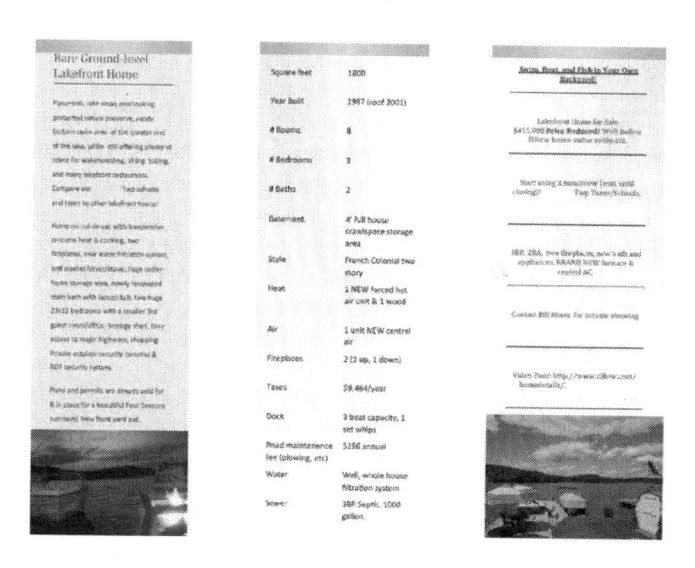

Figure 5-3 Tri-fold color brochure front.

> **TIP—Saving On Printing Costs**
>
> *Color brochures can be expensive. Don't print too many at a time—the information could change. It's an art to figure out how many to put in the box at one time. Not too many, in case someone grabs them all. You don't want to run out.*

Another lesson we learned was to give people as much information as possible. Many visitors were showing up without Realtors, and were not sure how to make an offer, let alone everything else involved in buying a home. We'll go into that in more detail in a later chapter, but the pertinent point for now is to provide some information to buyers about how to follow up with an offer, and perhaps business cards or a printed sheet that has contact information for local realty attorneys, inspectors, and finance officers.

I tried to find highly rated service providers, rather than just put random names on that list. For example, I asked our realty attorney "We already have the best in you, but whom else can we recommend to prospective buyers? Who do you like to work with?"

Chapter 5: Marketing: Putting It Out There

You can assemble all of this information into the "kit" that I mentioned earlier in this chapter. A page or half page that shows what a typical mortgage payment would be for several levels of down payments and mortgage rates would also be something useful to prospective buyers

Using Business Cards

Be creative in your marketing, you are in competition! We had color business cards made up with a few nice pictures and basic information. We included a line telling people to go to Zillow.com for more information. It wasn't that expensive to design these at staples.com or at the kiosk in the store. Bring a thumb/USB drive with your best pictures if you go to the store.

After we had our box of a few hundred of these business cards, we bought some sheets of blank labels and ran off stickers to put on the back of them. The stickers had more detailed information in black and white text.

I'm sure there was an option to do double-sided business cards and design that text on the back, but I missed it or didn't think of it at the time. Oh well, putting the stickers on a few hundred business cards was a fun family activity. We then placed these cards at strategic locations—events in the area, local pizza shops and restaurants, bulletin boards at shopping centers and grocery/convenience stores.

We always had the cards with us, to hand out wherever we went. It's amazing how many creative ways there are to work into a conversation with strangers that you have a home to sell. When we were at a conference at a swanky hotel in New York City, we were stealthily (we thought) placing small stacks around the hotel, when a very old woman appeared, seemingly out of nowhere.

"What are you doing?" she asked.

We thought we were busted. We sheepishly explained that we had a beautiful lake home to sell in New Jersey. It led to a conversation about how the woman's family was all 'water people' and they had been looking for a place to gather. She asked for some of the cards to take with her. Since she was draped in fur and expensive jewelry, we thought we had it made! We never heard from her again.

As you visit local establishments to ask permission to leave a stack of these at the register or on their bulletin boards, always ask for the manager. We always told them that if they refer a buyer to us, we'd pay them a $500 finder's fee, as long as we could verify that they were the ones that sent the folks to the house.

It's much less expensive than thousands of dollars in Realtor commissions, and it effectively puts people to work for you. Five hundred is a lot of money to your typical small business owner.

We visited marinas and boat dealers around the lake and asked them to talk up the convenience of having your own lakefront home and dock as opposed to all of the hassle of trailering their boat to the lake every time they wanted to go out on it. Don't limit this to just business people, make the same offer to neighbors and any others that you think might come in contact with people who might be looking.

TIP—Enlist an Army of Help

Find creative ways to get others to help you get the word out. Offer 'finders fees' or other types of incentives to anyone that finds you a buyer. It's far less expensive than paying a listing Realtor commission.

Social Marketing

We also asked friends and family to occasionally (not too often) put the link to our Zillow page on their Facebook and other social media pages, and possibly pass it along to their other contacts through email, bridge games, or whatever. Your friends may know the house well and be able to extoll its virtues, but don't ask so often that you become a pest. They may also be anxious to collect that $500 finder's fee.

Another idea that was surprisingly inexpensive was to pay to put our single-page ad in rotation for the huge electronic advertising signs that were in a local diner. We modified our brochure content into a single page document with one nice picture and very large text with just a couple of lines of the most important information. It had contact info, the open house hours, address, and "only 1.5 miles from where you sit." We only did this on weekends that we knew would be very busy, such as Memorial Day, 4th of July, and Labor Day. We also had a line on it to "take a business card on the way out" and made sure we had a stack of them by the diner exit.

Traditional Marketing—Newspapers

The old-school way of advertising the home for sale is the good old newspaper. As we keep saying, times have changed. We tried to ask each person who inquired about the house where they had heard about it, so that we could spend our marketing money wisely. I don't remember anyone saying they had seen it in the paper, and this was a widely circulated newspaper—The Newark Star Ledger.

We started out by putting a small ad in the Sunday real estate open house section. The papers make it difficult, at least the ones around us did. They want you to bundle in online postings (which were unnecessary, since we were already all over the Internet through MLS and our other websites), and reserve for some number of days or weeks. We found them difficult to deal with and expensive, compared to other ways to get the word out. No wonder the newspapers are dying out. They are yet another way of life that is being "Ubered."

Our survey revealed that by far most of our visitors had heard about the home on the Internet, while they were searching for properties that had the criteria they desired. I guess that makes sense. Would you want to waste time squinting at pages of tiny, cryptic real estate ads in the paper? Or would you rather get on an attractive website like Zillow and search based on your exact criteria, such as number of bedrooms, bathrooms, and waterfront and then having tons of nice pictures, maybe a video tour, and lots of information to view to narrow down the choices to visit?

Later in the process, we did place an ad in the New York Times Sunday paper, listing the home as a vacation property, since we had been getting some city folks who were interested in a weekend getaway. Amazingly, they were easier and more affordable than the other papers we had considered.

Preparing Your Website Pages

Because so many people today use the Internet instead of newspapers, our next section is very important. Let's talk about how to set up your website pages.

Zillow

We started with Zillow, since they seemed to be the most popular and had the best tools for setting up our page on their site. Most likely, Zillow already has a page on your home. If you've owned it for a long time, the information is probably inaccurate, as well as the corresponding estimate of the home's

Chapter 5: Marketing: Putting It Out There

worth. If you have bought it in the last few years, they probably have lots of detail, and even pictures. Make sure it's all correct!

Zillow also has a cool feature called "Make Me Move," where you can enter a price for your property that will entice you to move, even if you weren't planning to and don't want to officially list it for sale. This might be something good to do in order to drum up some interest while you are preparing everything else prior to listing.

We agreed that I am not going to give a complete tutorial on posting your home on Zillow or any of the other sites for that matter. That would encompass an entire book on its own, and of course would probably be out of date by the time the book published, since things change often in Internet-time. I will guide you through the high-level steps. The in-depth material and tutorials are readily available on the Internet in text or video form—find help by searching.

We also chose Zillow first because they have extensive help resources on the Internet, and a forum for asking questions. In the next chapter, we'll discuss a problem that occurred and how their email support people weren't very helpful, which is the normal case these days for just about any company.

The way the process works for these sites is that you first create an account on the website you want to post your page on. Then you can log in, and click that you want to post a home for sale by owner. It will ask you for the address, and then you may have to verify that you actually own the property. After that, you can enter some information about the house, your asking price, and upload your pictures.

To verify that you are the real owner on Zillow, they will show you a list of names and ask you to select your name from the list. The list is a randomly generated list with the name of the real owner (hopefully you!) inserted in it somewhere. They do this to prevent some random person from putting your home for sale on the site. Most likely they are using public records to find the name of the owner, as they do to find out other information such as prior listings, sales, and tax records. There is an area on the page to get help if there is a problem. For example, it might not show your name if you are a co-owner.

After the verification is resolved, take your time going through the various sections to set up your page. Make sure everything is accurate. I can imagine that you could get into serious trouble, or jeopardize your deal, if you have overstated or misstated any of the information. It can be a bit tricky knowing which home feature checkboxes to check off. Some of them can be ambiguous or vague. You can clarify anything that's unclear in the description and comments, or make notes to clarify certain items when you show the property. It can be confusing when it gets to things like square footage, since there's no definitive way to measure that.

Make sure that the pictures upload properly and display the way you want them. Again, choose your 'primary photo' carefully since this will show on thumbnail views in search results and alerts. Use captions if they are available, and write something enthusiastic and descriptive in them. Identify all rooms in the captions so that people don't get confused about which room is which in the pictures.

It might pay to get someone who is good with photography to take some quality pictures if you aren't comfortable creating them on your own. Realtors used to get photographers to do this, but I doubt many do these days, especially since most of us carry cameras in our pockets (smart phones and tablets) that are capable of high-resolution photography. Lighting and framing the shot are very important, and getting those just right are beyond the capabilities of most people.

Next, enter the title and description. There's quite a bit of space available, so organize your thoughts carefully and make sure that your spelling and grammar are correct. Be creative! For example, our home was brick, so we started with "Who was the smartest little pig? The one who lived in the brick house!"

Zillow Talk has a good chapter on how to best describe your house, including a statistical analysis of certain buzzwords. It discusses why you should avoid certain words that might sound like good choices, and how others can help you sell your home faster. I didn't get to read it until our story was almost over, but was happy to see that their analysis shows that longer descriptions sell more homes.

As we discussed in Chapter 3, "The Price is Right?" you should set up your own saved search on Zillow for houses in your area and in your price range. Look for examples that you like in that saved search of competing homes. You may want to now open the search criteria up to include homes for sale and not just sold homes.

Chapter 5: Marketing: Putting It Out There

This search will come in handy later in order to keep an eye on what's going on in the area and with your competitors. Zillow will notify you if any of the homes in that search group have a status change or if new homes are added. You can also mark homes as 'favorites' and Zillow will keep you updated via email, text, or app notification if anything changes with those.

Your headline or title text, for any of the websites that use one, should be eye-catching, not bland. For example, ours was "Swim, Fish, and Boat in Your Own Backyard!" It's just as important as the primary picture, as many prospective buyers will only see those two things in their search results. Be creative—think of something that teases and begs someone to open the link to learn more. Pull them in, but don't be obnoxious by doing things like using all capital letters or lots of exclamation points.

I really like that Zillow has a section called "What I Love About the Home." This is your chance to say what made the house a home to *you*. Talk about things like the great neighborhood, schools, or anything that stands out in your mind and makes your home better than the others in your area and price range.

When I mentioned the great schools in our township, many visitors remarked that their kids were grown. I always reminded them that it would be a factor when they later try to sell the home. In that way, I was indirectly steering them away from the competing lakefront homes in that other township, which had poorly rated schools.

Set your opening price in this section. You should have calculated that based on the advice in Chapter 3, "The Price is Right?"

In our case, a few days after we listed the house on Zillow, we had second thoughts about the price and a dropped it by $10,000. We worried that it might look bad to do that so soon, but then realized that each time we made a change, people who had favorited the house, or set up a search that included it were getting a notification about the change, so it was an unintentional, strategic move. Don't make price changes too often though, you don't want to come off as desperate.

WARNING—Erratic Price Changes

Be very steady at the wheel and avoid constant price changes. You may come off as desperate and disorganized to those who are watching. Be methodical. Once you go down, you can't (or shouldn't) go back up again.

Zillow allows you to put in a link to your home video tour. This is highly recommended. You can hire someone to do a home video tour, and even commission aerial and inside drone tours. We priced that out and it was too expensive for us to consider. I will admit to making an attempt to use this as an excuse to justify a drone purchase, which was quickly shot down (the idea not the drone).

Google is coming out with new technology soon that will allow you to create a 3D tour of your home by using an app on your phone or tablet. They already have the "street view" on Google Maps that allow someone to view the actual home and surrounding neighborhood from outside. If your neighborhood is nice, you might advertise this, as long as your area is one that Google has done this in.

We opted for taking our own video camera through the home just as if we were giving someone a tour during an open house. It wasn't the greatest, but it was inexpensive and actually kind of homey and personal. This is a great tool to have for people that call and can't make it to your open house. They can tour it on the Internet, in the convenience of their own home.

There is also a place on your Zillow page to put a link to the website for the home, if you have one. We really didn't think it was necessary to create our own website, since we were going to have pages on all of these other realty sites. We did use the opportunity to put a link in this space to download a PDF file of our brochure. You can put the brochure PDF file on any number of file-sharing websites, such as Dropbox, Google Drive, and Microsoft OneDrive. If you have a Google, Microsoft or other type of account (which just about everyone does), you probably have some amount of free storage that comes with it. Just put the file there and provide a link to it in this space on Zillow and other websites.

Zillow doesn't make it easy for people that are in our situation, which is essentially that we are selling the home ourselves, but have a flat fee MLS listing. They are still kind of stuck in that world where you are either FSBO or MLS, and this new

Chapter 5: Marketing: Putting It Out There

area is a grey area between the two. If you say that it's on MLS, they assume you are a Realtor and want information that you probably don't have, and you may lose control of editing the site since they will depend on the dreaded feed of junk from MLS for information about the property.

So we posted as for sale by owner, but included the MLS number prominently in the description and 'Other Information' areas, so that any Realtors who saw the listing knew that we were already listed and that we would honor their sell-side commission. Another reason we did it this way was that as soon as you post a FSBO ad, be prepared for an onslaught of phone calls, texts, and emails from friendly Realtors who are offering to help you by listing your home. Telling them that you are already on MLS makes them go away quickly.

Zillow will complement the information that you have provided with all kinds of other stuff that they will insert on your page. They are paid by Realtors to place the Realtor contact information on the page, along with your own information. I wish they didn't do that, but they have to make their money some way! Zillow also places links for buyers to calculate what the mortgage would be, links for similar homes for sale, similar homes that have already sold, information about the area, school ratings, historical and current listings, sales and tax rates for the property, and how many people have viewed and favorited the property.

This is all very important and fascinating information about the home and it's amazing how much data Zillow can suck out of the Internet. It's fantastic information for buyers to look through. If your schools aren't highly rated, you might want to put something in your text about the great private schools in the area, or about any cooperative agreements with other public school districts. If the taxes are high, make sure to extoll all of the great things you get in that township for those tax dollars.

Zillow's Infamous Zestimate

The most important and controversial item on the page is the infamous "Zestimate," which is Zillow's calculated estimate of what the property is worth. This is based on the information that you enter, as well as the other data they pull in, as well as certain analytic information, such as what Zillow considers to be the comparable homes in the area.

It's maddening to watch this number go up and down for no apparent reason, kind of like watching your stock portfolio during good and bad times. At least the reasons behind stock fluctuations are known.

Chapter 5: Marketing: Putting It Out There

It's very difficult to discern why the Zestimate changes and Zillow is very tight-lipped about their algorithm. Ours went from pretty low in the winter, to very high in the summer, then down again in the fall. I can only guess that this has something to do with it being a waterfront property, and perhaps the interest (page views) being higher during those prime summer months.

Realtors will dismiss the Zestimate as useless. When I did some research to try to find out what data is used to come up with this number, I found that it is more accurate in some places than others. This is because not all townships, counties, and states report data the same, or as accurately. In some counties, such as ours, the Zestimate is very accurate in terms of what a house will ultimately sell for.

Checking the Zestimate for your competitive homes is another way to see if your price is in line with where it should be. We made sure to advertise the disparity prominently when the Zillow estimate was well above our asking price! I have another theory that Zillow's computers were watching our price drops and when we marked it as 'Pending offer' it started dropping its Zestimate down to make the Zestimate look accurate by the time the house closed.

> **WARNING—Don't Lose It All**
>
> *All of the work you are putting into these sites is not saved on your computer. It can all go away in a flash, as it did for us. Make sure you are saving your pictures and text on your own computer as a backup. And back up your computer!*

When you have your Zillow site set up just the way you want it, please save the information immediately. Copy the pictures you used to a folder on your computer named 'zillow' and copy any text and links into a document and save it. Maybe put the order of the pictures in the file names.

We also printed the entire Zillow page to a PDF document. Most computers have a utility installed that will let you print to a PDF file instead of a real printer, and this is very useful. If you don't see this option, you might want to install the CutePDF utility or another like it.

And by the way, make sure you are backing your computer up. It's very possible that the information could be overwritten and lost. As you will see, this happened to us and was just one of many small disasters that we hope to save you from with this book. You can simply back this data up to an inexpensive USB thumb drive. Just don't lose the thumb drive!

Postlets

After all of the above was done, we spent some time admiring our sweet Zillow page and then asked "What's next?" There are a ton of real estate sites out there, and we certainly wanted to be on other popular ones like Zillow, Craigslist, and Yahoo Real Estate. But we sure didn't want to have to do all of that work again for every other site. Fortunately, we found out about a site called Postlets.com. Postlets will allow you to enter information in one place and then they shoot it out to a bunch of other popular sites, including some of the ones we mentioned and wanted to be on, and more. What a great, timesaving solution to the problem!

Postlets is owned by Zillow. We created an account and set up the site similar to the way we had Zillow set up. There are some things missing in Postlets that are in Zillow, but it's close enough and a pretty nice site. You have to remember to renew your listing every sixty days or so, but Postlets will remind you.

Copy your text from the Zillow page (or your saved document) and use the same pictures. Postlets doesn't have a "Why I Love the Home" section, but you can copy that in from the Zillow page to create your own. When you get to the final step and click the Promote button, the magic happens and your page is sent out to every site on their list. It may take a little time to actually show up.

We had become worried that this would overwrite our Zillow site, but it never did. I assume that is because we had already taken control of the Zillow page ourselves and set it up, and it must have recognized that and locked it from any change other than those we made ourselves. But as I said, back it up just in case!

Craigslist

A very cool feature of Postlets is that it shows you the HTML code for the page that you created, so that you can copy and paste it into other places if you want. HTML is a computer markup language that allows you to describe how you want the data you are entering laid out on the page. For example, which words are bold, and where headings are. Postlets doesn't post to Craigslist as one of its regular sites, but you will see an option to Post to Craigslist, which you have to do manually. This is shown in Figure 5-4.

Chapter 5: Marketing: Putting It Out There

Figure 5-4 Postlets export options.

Since I was already familiar with Craigslist, having sold most of our homeowner possessions on it recently, I preferred to copy the HTML code and paste it into the Craigslist ad that I created by myself. I'm sure it would work well either way, and there are specific instructions on how to do this on the Postlets help section online. Postlets has a tool for creating a flyer from the information you provided. We didn't try this, but it is an alternative if you don't have mad skills or tools for desktop publishing.

Speaking of Craigslist, it may be a bit daunting for you, given that the site has a reputation for seediness. We definitely got some of the more unusual candidates from there, but do not look past it as a source of potential buyers. It is a very widely viewed site, and the real estate ads are not really the area of concern. Like any site, you may get emails, calls, or texts from trolls after putting your page up.

Make sure to keep an eye on your Craigslist page. It requires you to renew every few days. It's easy to do, just click the 'Renew' link, but you won't get any notice that it is due. I always kept open tabs in my browser for all of the pages I was using, just in case something like this happened. Most browsers have a setting to remember those tabs, and reopen them each time you launch the browser.

Flat-Fee and MLS Site Content

The last thing we had to do was to set up the MLS listing info on the website provided by Realmart Realty, the flat-fee MLS company that we had chosen. Fortunately, Realmart has a very usable site, which is kind of rare for these smaller outfits (compared to Zillow) and something that you should definitely factor into your choice when selecting a flat-fee provider.

The problem however, is with the MLS system. You are restricted in the number of pictures, type of pictures, and text. You are constrained to a little over eight hundred characters for your MLS description. No wonder the Realtors all rely on that horrible shorthand notation they use. So you have to carefully analyze your nice, lengthy, descriptive Zillow narrative and boil it down to the bare essentials.

MLS is restrictive in that they won't let you post any links, in case you got the wise idea to just put a link to your Zillow page in there. You cannot include your phone number or personal email. Don't even think about posting a picture of your Zillow page (yeah, we tried that). A portion of the Realmart page for entering in the MLS and Realtor.com descriptions is shown in Figure 5-5.

108 Show and Sell: Selling Your Home Today

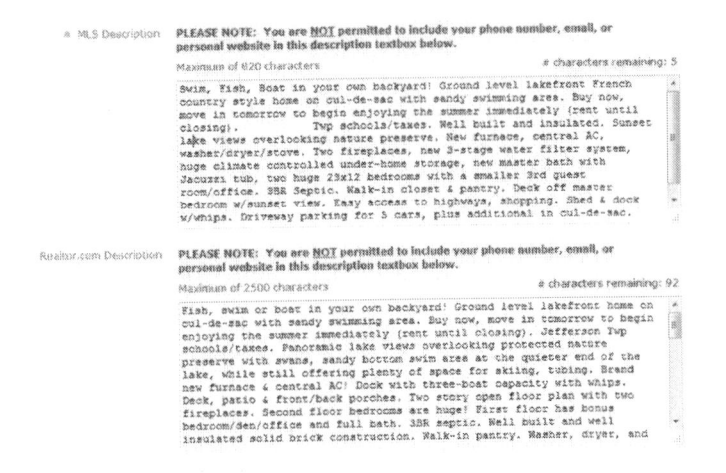

Figure 5-5 Realmart fields for entering MLS and Realtor.com descriptions.

Everything you enter goes through your flat-fee listing real estate brokerage before publishing, so make sure to choose one that is responsive (and not just responsive during the part where they are trying to get your money).

Many flat-fee companies allow you to post on Realtor.com as part of their base package or as an extra. It may happen automatically, as part of the MLS aggregation that Realtor.com does. This is a good thing, as there are television and other commercials for Realtor.com and a lot of people use it when searching for homes. Realtor.com is part of the MLS former monopoly though, so it has similar restrictions, depending on the MLS. As you can see in Figure 5-5, ours allowed a "whopping" 2500 character description field, which still pales in comparison to more modern realty sites.

A problem that we quickly encountered after setting up our MLS info was that we got a friendly email from Realmart saying that someone had complained that we had "broken the MLS rules" and used pictures from a previous MLS listing. We assume that perhaps a Realtor had seen the listing, someone who was familiar with the property, and took umbrage at our efforts to sell our home this way.

U.S. and international laws protect the originators of content, which can be written words, pictures, etc. Be careful about reusing anyone else's stuff. You may be breaking the law and violating a copyright. It may never be detected in minor cases, but be aware that using previous MLS pictures is against the rules and frowned upon by the establishment. Local Realtors will most certainly notice that you have reused their pictures. We didn't know this and had to quickly switch gears and take our own photos, which were of empty rooms by that time. However, this led us to the fantastic option of having the photos virtually staged, as shown in Figures 4-1 and 4-2 in Chapter

4, "Prepping: Empty Nest Syndrome." Problem solved!

Another problem was that around mid-June our beautiful Zillow page was suddenly all messed up. Remember when we couldn't figure out why the MLS wasn't overwriting it? It turns out there was some kind of glitch, and when the glitch was fixed the terse MLS data flowed in and overwrote all of our carefully created pictures and text. One day it was all there, the next day it was all gone. This is why backups of everything are necessary. Each time we restored it from our saved data, MLS overwrote it again.

It took days to fix the problem. The solution was for wonderful and efficient Nancy at Realmart to notify Zillow that we had their permission to put up the page independent of the MLS feed, which Zillow then turned off. The down side of this is that to make it happen, your page on Zillow has to be marked as For Sale by Owner. This is another reason to make sure the MLS number is in the text description and Other Information fields so that Realtors and buyers can see it.

Chapter 5: Marketing: Putting It Out There

> **TIP—Check Your Pages Daily**
>
> *Keep all of your web pages loaded up in different tabs of your Internet browser, and make sure it's set to remember and load your tabs each time you run the browser. Check every day to ensure that your pages are showing correctly.*

Ebay and Other Listing Sites

We had heard that eBay has a real estate area for auctions and regular classified-type home for sale listings. We took a look at it, and decided it wasn't for us.

We believe that using our approach, as far as which websites we used, gave us the best of all worlds for the least amount of effort. There are many other websites that will let you post listings, but we chose to stay with the primary ones, so that we didn't have a slew of them to maintain when we made changes. When we had to make a change, we made it on Zillow, Postlets, Craigslist, and the Realmart MLS site.

Other Marketing Options and Approaches

There are many other options for marketing your home. We placed a guest book at the entrance for our open houses, with a note to leave some contact information in order to be notified of price changes or other updates. That old-school approach didn't work out too well. People were usually in a hurry or felt uncomfortable with it. We failed to recognize it as an outdated approach.

As we've made clear, there are much easier ways for buyers to get these kinds of updates, such as by flagging a home as one of your favorites on the many websites that carry listings. If you have a website for your home, there is a great tool called MailChimp (http://mailchimp.com/) that allows you to maintain email lists and use them for marketing.

There are also call-capture hotlines that you can sign up for. These allow you to set up a 24-hour recording about your house that people can listen to when they dial a toll-free number and enter your special house ID. Some people may be more likely to do this than call you directly, since they don't have to talk to a real human being. These services will also provide you with the phone numbers of people who called it, so that you can then reach out

Chapter 5: Marketing: Putting It Out There

to them directly. I can imagine people being annoyed at that.

It sounded like an outdated approach to us, and yet another thing to pay for. But if you work all day and can't take calls, and want to have a dedicated voice mail greeting to provide some info about the house, this might be a good option. Your existing voice mail and phone system probably allow you to put in menu prompts to "Press one for information about our home for sale, all others press any other digit." Many people no longer have home phone lines (we didn't), so check to see if your mobile phone carrier has this capability, or use one of these dedicated services.

"Back in the day" they also had those radio-frequency gizmos where you can tune into a special radio station in your car to listen to a recorded message when you are within close proximity to the house.

That was probably interesting back before people started driving and walking around with mobile phones. Everything is "on demand" now. People are impatient and want the path of least resistance to information. A lot of people probably don't even know how to operate their car radios today, with satellite, Bluetooth, and other new technologies providing the music and news, weather and traffic. That's why we chose to put high quality, descriptive brochures within arm's reach (without getting out of the car) that contained our phone number, email address, and web site addresses for additional pictures and info.

There are other approaches, like using Google Adwords to make your house more prominent in general searches. You have to pick your battles, as each of these involves time and your wallet or purse. I'm sure that as time goes by, and more and more technology becomes available, there will be additional creative ways to market your property.

Summary

If you have been following along so far, and have taken the steps I have prescribed, you are probably finally ready to "put it out there" and list your house. There is some conventional logic as to the timing of this. For example, some wise sages say that it's best to list on a Thursday morning, as that's when prospective home buyers are getting ready to organize their weekend visits.

That sounds logical, but keep in mind that some sites will make your listing immediately available, while others, such as MLS, may take a day or more. Factor that into your timing for each

Chapter 5: Marketing: Putting It Out There

site. Just be sure you're ready! I'd also wait until you are ready to have an open house the weekend just after your house goes live on these sites, and maybe the following weekends.

In the next chapter, we'll discuss what comes next. You will put your listing out there, and hopefully start receiving calls, emails, texts, carrier pigeons, and every possible kind of inquiry. You have to set up open houses and private tours of the house. These first few weeks are a very critical time. This is where the fun really starts. Now you have to engage with actual humans, and put your selling ability to the test. Prepare to meet your potential buyers!

6 Show and Sell

If you've followed our steps to this point, your price is correctly calculated, you've got the place looking fabulous, and you have a marketing machine fired up and humming along. Now it's time to show and sell.

Getting Ready to Show

Your home should be in tip-top shape, brochures at the ready and conveniently displayed, as well as the other auxiliary information that we discussed earlier. You should have a complete "buyer's kit" with information about the area, finance officers, realty attorneys, sample mortgage payments for current fixed and variable rates with several levels of down payments, how to make an offer, and other helpful information.

I had our last years' worth of utility bills at the ready. People will always ask about those, so it's good to show proof. Always factor in any unique conditions. Let them know that their mileage may vary. For example, for some months we were both at home every day and our utility bills would have been less if we had been away working in the office.

Zillow shows the last few years' worth of property taxes, but it might not hurt to have proof of those handy as well, as it's another frequent question. Your brochure or fact sheet should show all room dimensions. Hopefully, your visitors will go home and start measuring their furniture to see how it fits.

You might also want to fill out a standard property disclosure statement and have copies to hand out. Those are required with any home sale, so you might as well do it now. It is a series of pages with checkboxes and questions about the home, such as how old the roof is. Blank forms can be found and downloaded from many Internet sites, at realty offices, or from realty attorneys.

There are Internet sites that will sell you a complete package of all forms needed for a home sale and closing, but be very careful about playing attorney on your own. We preferred to have our attorney handle the legal business.

> **TIP—Practice Makes Perfect**
>
> *Before receiving your first visitors, make sure to rehearse your tour with someone else. Keep a list of talking points for each room and feature. Use this same tour to create your video tour, and post the link to it on your website pages.*

Conventional wisdom says that you should bake bread in the oven to make the home smell homey. A lot of people use candles and other types of scented air fresheners. This can be viewed by visitors as an attempt to cover up other kinds of unpleasant odors, and it might set off allergies or other problems with sensitivity to smells. It's best to go with something extremely light, or just clean and natural in terms of scents. It may be a good idea to have some Febreeze spray handy though, in case something completely unexpected and unfortunate occurs, as it did to us a few times!

As I discussed in the last chapter, make the house as neutral as possible in areas such as religious, sports, or politics. Remove your family photos so that they can visualize themselves in the home more easily. If it's winter, think about putting up some pictures of the exterior from spring, summer or fall.

For our first few open houses, we did have some soft classic rock or jazz music playing, but we found that even when played at low volume it was distracting. Another cardinal rule is to keep the toilet seats down and all waste containers empty.

> **WARNING—Be Covered**
>
> *Strangers will be in your house. Some will do strange things, like hang out of a window to try to examine the roof. Make sure your homeowner and umbrella policies are up to date!*

Take care with your personal documents, information and belongings. We even had Realtors, who should know better, rummage through our drawers and pull out documents that we had there for our own reference. We had some local magazines handy for people to browse through, and to show the many things to do in the area, and some folks took them home as freebies. We started to tape things to the display counter to avoid this, and put signs saying "Take one" for the things we really wanted them to take, such as the brochures. It can be confusing to people.

Avoid having any of your own pets or kids present, as they tend to be unpredictable when you can't afford it. You never know how they will interact with those of your guests, who may turn out to be the instigators and provoke an unfortunate reaction. Yes, people will actually bring their pets "so they can see the house too."

> **WARNING—Pets and Kids**
>
> *Try to avoid having your pets and kids present for showings, and be prepared for anything if your visitors bring theirs. Both can be very unpredictable.*

You should have acquired a lockbox so that Realtors can show the home when you aren't home (by appointment only, of course). The lockbox has a compartment that can be opened with a combination. The compartment contains a key to open the home. Realtors have ones that can be opened electronically, and track which Realtors showed the house and when. You can buy a combination lockbox on sites like Amazon.com, or it may be offered as an extra by your flat-fee Realtor, if you use one.

On open house days, make sure the home can be clearly identified by folks driving around looking for it. It's nice to spend a few bucks on a couple of helium balloons and tie them to the sign out front.

Security Precautions

Realtors will tell you that this is where it gets scary, and to some extent, they are correct. You are now in a position where you are going to have to allow complete strangers into your home and that can be a bit daunting. In our case, the home was vacant, so I didn't have a problem with letting Realtors and even the occasional prospective home buyer in when we weren't there. We carefully vetted the home buyers first, of course.

> **WARNING—Security**
>
> *Take any and all precautions for your safety. There are ways to vet your visitors in advance of any appointment to show the home.*

We had security cameras around the exterior of the house, so any comings and goings were recorded. This certainly would deter someone who intended any kind of wrongdoing. If I had ever felt uncomfortable, I would have been sure to mention that to visitors, as well as the fact that the recordings were stored in the cloud, not on some laptop or DVR in the home that could be removed by a perpetrator.

We always did some degree of vetting before we agreed to meet someone at the house. You can get a good feel for someone simply by asking the questions you should be asking to any prospective buyer, such as why they are moving, where they are moving from, do they have a mortgage prequalification, and so forth. Do not rely solely on email conversations, always at a minimum talk to the person on the phone.

You can ask for their ID in advance, as well as any paperwork that identifies them, and perhaps even do an Internet search on their names. There are Internet sites like Spokeo.com that will give you an amazing amount of information about someone for a price, but be careful—some of them are scams.

Your degree of comfort in this area as well as factors such as the crime rate in your area should drive the precautions that you take, including whether you are comfortable showing the home yourself at all. If that's the case, then listing with a full-service Realtor may be a better option for you.

Other safety precautions are things like having pepper spray handy, only showing during daylight hours when neighbors or others are around, leaving windows open so that any call for help is audible, and having someone there with you at all times. I've never heard of people getting attacked while showing homes, but I'm sure it happens, and this is something that Realtors have to worry about all the time, which is why they always vet their customers before showing them around.

Always think ahead, be safe, and don't take chances—we live in a dangerous world. By all means, if you are not comfortable, it's probably better to let a Realtor handle everything. You can save a lot by selling your home on your own, but money should never be put ahead of safety. And flat-fee companies like Realmart have options available to handle all of this for far less than the 3% a regular listing agent would charge.

Handling Inquiries and Scammers

After we made our web pages active, we started to receive a lot of email inquiries that seemed to be bogus. Always be on alert when someone offers to buy something without actually looking at it. There are all kinds of scams involving Paypal, Western Union, and other forms of payment. For any inquiries that sounded suspicious, we gave them our lawyer's information and told them to go to him with their offer, since we knew he'd take all of the proper steps to vet them. Just hearing the word 'lawyer' scared them off; we would usually hear nothing further.

Running an Open House

Prior to our first open house, we were preparing the home and I was very concerned about parking. Where were we going park all of these excited people coming to buy our home? What if a fight breaks out, like on black Friday shopping, between overzealous buyers? We had parking for about six cars. I put up signs pointing people to overflow parking areas. Of course, I was being overly optimistic. Overflow parking would never be required.

The guidance from Realtors and the books I had read said that during an open house, you'll get four to five different groups of visitors on a good day. Typical open house times are 1-4pm on Sundays. That seems to be something that Realtors either formally or informally agree or perhaps they even collude on. However, we didn't have to follow any Realtor rules. We set ours up for 1-5pm, a bit longer than most, and it was definitely a good strategy. A lot of our traffic arrived in that last hour, and in fact we often had people show up as we were closing up shop around 5pm. They were probably coming from the ones that shut down earlier.

The first hour or so was usually pretty quiet—nobody wants to be the first one to a party. In hindsight, it probably would have been better to do 2-5pm or even 3-5pm, but in reality I was always at the house much earlier to cut the grass and make sure everything was ready.

Conventional wisdom says not to have open houses on Saturdays or on holiday weekends. Again, we were the rebels and broke all of those rules. The Realtors warned me that nobody would show up, and I was wasting a perfectly good weekend. Well, the lakefront house wasn't a bad place to spend a weekend anyway, and we hoped we would drive traffic by being unconventional. This strategy worked well. Apparently people don't mind visiting open houses on holiday weekends, because we had good traffic during those dates. I'm sure we drove all of the Realtors and competing homeowners crazy trying to keep up with us. If you only get one visitor, that may be the lucky one. And the bonus is that it forces you to keep the house clean!

Make sure to accurately advertise your open house on all of your websites and marketing materials. You might provide incentives, like a drawing for a gift card to a local restaurant. We decided not to do this because we thought it would just bring a lot of folks who wanted in for the drawing, but had no intention to buy a home.

Each week, around Wednesday or Thursday, I would update our Zillow, Craigslist, Realmart/MLS, and Postlets sites with the open house dates for that coming weekend. It's probably better to do this later in the week, so that the notifications go out just as people are getting ready to plan their weekends. No matter what day I did it, Zillow was great about sending reminders on the weekend to anyone who had saved the house as a favorite or part of a saved search.

TIP—Open House Advertising

Make sure that all of your Internet pages have the correct info for your open houses. Post it around mid-week, so they can broadcast it to their home followers.

My routine on open house days was to get to the house early, post the directional signs at the strategic intersections in the area, turn all of the lights on, run all of the faucets (since the home had been sitting for a while), put out snacks, cut the grass, and then visually inspect every room and outside area to be sure it all looked great. I always brought plenty of things to keep myself busy, and in fact kept the Internet service on at the house so I could work and use my laptop while I waited. This was also helpful for guests to keep their kids occupied, and to do any searches for information that they requested while there.

One of the first visitors we had, even before the first open house, made a cash offer on the spot for $410,000. Since this was well under what we thought the house should sell for, and it was our first few days on the market, we declined. There were a few other factors, such as the guy coming off like he was right out of Tony Soprano's mob gang. I was worried about getting mixed up with him and ending up at the bottom of the lake in cement overshoes, as they say in the Jimmy Cagney movies. I don't want to spoil the ending of our story, but I would later second-guess that decision.

You should turn on all interior lights for maximum brightness during your open house. It's distracting to keep turning them on as you enter each room, then off as you exit when showing the home. It could also cause a bulb to blow out at the wrong time. Put out some bowls of snacks, and have bottled water or other refreshments available. Keep in mind that some people will show up with their kids, so consider the 'messiness' factor of anything you provide. For example, chocolate and soda may not be a good idea.

What to Expect When Visitors Arrive

Speaking of kids, when people bring them, they will likely run wild through your house and start fighting over the bedrooms. Don't expect the adults to do much about it. Kids being kids, they are capable of all kinds of mayhem.

A couple brought their kids to our open house, and they proceeded to tickle our well trained Bishon mercilessly, until she urinated slightly on the carpet, something she has never done before. The kids screamed in horror and the adults reacted with disgust and left. Be prepared for anything when there are kids (or adults) in the picture.

One Sunday, I noticed an older man wandering around the front of the house with one of our brochures in his hand. I invited him in (always a good idea, some folks are shy) and gave him a tour of the home. As I always did, I asked him if he would like a cold bottled water from the fridge. He asked if I had anything stronger. I did have a left-over six pack of beer, and offered him one of those.

Big mistake! He proceeded to sit down at the dining room table and chat about his life story, politics, and life in general while asking for beer after beer. As other people showed up to look at the house, he began introducing himself to them and chatting them up. My puzzled visitors looked to me for an explanation, and I could only shrug. He was a nice fellow, so it wasn't that bad, and of course when the beer was gone he thanked me and said he had to be off to a party at the VFW.

So in fact he had probably had no intention to buy a house, and was just using our place and stash to pregame for his party. Perhaps he saw the movie *The Wedding Crashers*, and decided to become an Open House Crasher.

Some people may drop by to see if there's any good eats, and some who drop by may actually be the people who are selling competitive homes, or their Realtors. Always be careful what you say.

Don't be frustrated when people come by and waste your time. It's just part of the game, and Realtors have to deal with this in spades. Some folks apparently just like to drive around and visit open houses, especially those in scenic areas like our lakefront. You never know when one of those people will mention it to a viable buyer at work or any of their social circles, so always treat them the same as anyone else.

As I said, some folks can be shy, so keep an eye out front for folks that may stop and grab a brochure. This would often happen prior to the official start of the open house, or on days that I was there when there wasn't even an open house scheduled. Simply opening the door and inviting them in for a tour in a friendly and cheerful voice can work wonders.

Organizing and Giving Your Home Tour

You should have a mental checklist to run through as you give each party a tour of the home. As you enter each room, don't say boring things like "This is the living room." Point out unique features, such as "A great feature of this living room is the fireplace insert, which unlike most fireplaces, which send the heat up the chimney, will distribute warm, clean air into the room," or "we loved to hang out in this family room and enjoy the natural light and fresh air breeze from the many windows."

Practice these points for each area of the home and property so you don't forget them. Offer refreshments as you greet people, and at the end of the tour. Point out what's in the buyer's packet, and encourage them to come back or think about contacting you if they might want to put in an offer. By all means ask where they found out about the home, so you can more properly use your marketing dollars.

At the conclusion of your tour, always ask them if they would like to go through the home a second time on their own while you wait outside. I didn't like asking this at the start because I always wanted to be able to point out the features they may have otherwise missed. Ask them what their favorite and least favorite features were. Just asking the questions will get people to open up and disclose valuable information.

In our case, we realized that almost every potential buyer loved the house, but were concerned about the empty lots across the street, which had badly overgrown weeds and were owned by a neighbor. It was such a constant concern that we had to do something. Too many of our potential buyers said it was a showstopper because they were worried about insects and animals using it as a haven. It was pretty ugly and a community eyesore and our other neighbors had also expressed concern about it.

I contacted the neighbor, who lived a few houses down the road and also owned a mobile home community nearby with her husband. She said they were planning on developing the lots and leasing them for twenty five years to people to buy and put modular homes on them. I didn't quite get the logic in that or why anyone would want to buy a home and put it on rented property, but didn't get into that with her. I was a bit nervous approaching her about it, because she had a reputation for being controlling and nasty to the other neighbors, but as we hadn't been there that long we hadn't seen that side of her. "Beware the Trailer Park Queen!" the other neighbors said. "Don't poke the bear! The troll will come out of her cave and pillage the village!"

I couldn't believe that someone could be so horrible, so I asked her politely if she could please clean the lots up, as we were getting a lot of negative comments from potential buyers.

The Trailer Park Queen responded by spewing an incredible amount of hatred and vitriol in my direction—a barrage of childish, immature, and frankly horrible text messages and threats. She demanded that we remove our boat trailer from another of their nearby overgrown lots by noon the next day. We had been paying them for the storage for years, and she and her husband had both said that we could keep it there until we moved, as long as it was before the fall, when they would start storing boats again.

We moved the trailer and went to the township to see if they could help. There are township laws about property maintenance, but this one fell through a loophole because there weren't homes on the lots yet. So we were left to deflect by pointing out to our visitors that "With the beautiful lake view out back, who's going to spend any time looking out front?" Our philosophy is to always make lemonade from lemons, and by all means to avoid feeding trolls, and so we moved on.

We had a neighbor on one side who occasionally liked to play his music loud outdoors on the weekend, and asked him if he could avoid that during our open house times, and he kindly obliged, as any good neighbor would. The moral of the story here is to always survey your surroundings, and the things that may or may not be out of your control, and do what you can. Have a plan in place to explain things to concerned buyers. We were always honest about the negatives as well as the positives when showing the house. Maybe that's why it took so long to sell!

> **TIP—Patrol Regularly**
>
> *Between showings at your open house, patrol the inside and outside of the home carefully. Things can change quickly.*

Handling Private and Realtor Showings

There were three types of showings—we showed it privately, the Realtors showed it, and we showed it during open houses. Realtors would call or email us and ask to show the house, since we were the listed contact on MLS. Sometimes they would call the flat-fee agency (Realmart), who would direct them to us. Either way, we would make sure to fill them in about the house and the important talking points, and ask them to please read our Zillow ad before showing the house.

I found that Realtors would avoid Zillow and its content, and steer their clients away from that kind of site. Zillow and sites like it are the devil to them, they live in a world where MLS has always been king. Those sites threaten their way of life. They would faithfully show up with their printout of the crappy MLS page and give that to their clients. Some Realtors would even come prior to their showing and hide our materials in order to limit what their clients were exposed to. Sigh.

We would take note of when the Realtors planned on bringing their clients to the house, so that we could avoid the awkward situation of two showing up at the same time. We then gave the Realtor the lockbox combination to get in, and made a note to check in with them after the visit.

We always asked them to follow up with us, but most would not until we followed up ourselves, so be proactive. If you trust some prospective buyers enough, you could also give them the lockbox combo to let themselves in for a private tour, but of course if you have all of your things in the house this would probably not be a good idea. If it's vacant like ours was, there wasn't as much risk, other than liability if someone should get hurt, so always make sure your insurance is up to date.

Regular folks who are not Realtors are much less likely to return the lights and other things to the way they were when they arrived, and not as likely to put the key back into the lockbox, so be sure to check everything after their visit. After you read the rest of the stories in this chapter, you'll see why we rarely gave the lockbox combo to anyone who was not a Realtor.

People warned us that Realtors would steer clients away from for sale by owner or flat-fee listed homes like ours, and we have no way of knowing if that happened, but I refused to believe that any Realtor would walk away from a large commission and chance to sell any home for those reasons. It was our experience that the younger Realtors had gotten the memo, hello—the world is changing, and they very cooperative, while some of the older ones would bring their clients there somewhat grudgingly, and either ask questions or make comments that showed their ignorance and disapproval of us doing things the way we were.

Amazing but True Stories

As the weekends went by and the spring gave way to summer, things were either very dull or very exciting. The dull times weren't so bad. I'd pull out a lawn chair from the shed and work on my tan, catch up on my reading, listen to some good music out by the lake, maybe take the boat out for a spin within view of the house in case someone came by.

As I said, we were selling the boat too (with the mention that it came with an optional lakefront house). We had positioned the boat as part of a turnkey deal with the house, for those that yearned for the lakefront experience, to save them the hassle of buying the house and then have to go boat shopping.

One fellow who I'll call "The Chef" came by with his four kids, who ran amuck throughout the property while I showed him the house. He was extremely excited about the home, and wanted the boat with it as a package deal. He kept psyching the kids up big-time about the house. "You guys want to live on the lake?" "YEAH, DADDA!"

The pep-rally yelling and screaming went on and on. It became apparent he was doing this for a reason—the primary decision-maker in the family, Mama, was not present and they had to go home to her to make their case. He came back the next day, with Mama and the kids in tow. Mama proceeded to let him know in no uncertain terms that the house was beyond their means, and it was clear that Mama was the person in charge of that family unit. She also wanted a basement, which we didn't have.

Not to be deterred, the next weekend The Chef called and asked if he could test drive the boat. I agreed, and the following weekend he showed up, again with his wound-up hyperactive kids, which I hadn't counted on. I asked about his boating experience, which he espoused, and then I handed him the keys and we all boarded the vessel.

Chapter 6: Show and Sell   139

The first thing he did was to try to back out without raising the trim (prop) and raked it against the bottom, as the lake was still at low-water spring stage. After we worked out of that debacle, he clumsily navigated the boat around, learning on the job, I began to suspect since I had to show him where the controls were and how they worked. The kids, all bundled up in life vests, were going wild. He ventured into a few shallow areas, despite my warnings, and bottomed out, and I was starting to get upset.

The next few hours turned into what was apparently a pre-planned free evening on the boat for him and his kids, as he slowly took them around on this "test drive" to all of the coves and areas around the nine-mile long lake. As it started to get dark, I had to shut him down and request that we get back. No, we can't stop for ice cream, kids. He got out and enthusiastically said he would be in touch the next day. He did call, and...wait for it...you guessed it...Mama said no.

The Chef was a persistent man. I next heard from him when he called me the week before Father's Day weekend to say that Mama had reconsidered, and asked if they could all move into the house for the holiday weekend and use the house and boat to "see if they liked it and make a final decision." I told him essentially "Yeah, that's not going to happen." Fool me once...

The moral here is to not be too paranoid, but always be ready to second guess people's intentions. We had a lot of visitors who just enjoyed driving around looking at lakefront houses. It was dismaying to spend so much time with them and hear them blatantly saying things like "Hey honey, maybe if we hit the lottery we can afford something like this someday." But again, they could always be the one to tell someone who can afford it about the house. Or, maybe they would hit the lottery, you just never know.

Eventually a couple came and they loved the boat and house. They could not afford the house, but bought the boat. To seal the deal, I told them that they could continue to dock the boat at the house, to save them the exorbitant dock fees that most marinas charge. It was a nice thing to do, because I thought they would have bought it anyway—it was a very good deal and a very nice boat. It helped us, because the boat sure looked enticing out there to our prospective home buyers. It exemplified lakefront living.

In the following weeks, it did suck to see them come and walk past me working on my tan in the backyard and gleefully load up the boat and take it

Chapter 6: Show and Sell 141

out for a nice day on the lake. But these were genuinely nice people, and the guy gave me an old lawnmower to use, which was really great, since I had overzealously sold our nice Toro and had been paying others to cut the grass, since the house was probably going to be sold before the grass needed to be cut again. Win-win!

This is where we get to the part of the book that could be a bit offensive. These "crappy" stories need to be told because there is a moral in each one. You need to know what you could be getting into if you want to show your own home.

One fine summer day, a well-to-do couple came from the big city. They were Manhattanites, and the woman was very enthusiastic about the place. She said she wanted to have a place for her young kids to enjoy nature on their weekends away from the city. She raved at every turn as I showed her around the house. Her husband, whose name was Armando or something exquisite like that, seemed to be bouncing around on the balls of his feet a lot. He clearly was uncomfortable about something, and was urging his wife to wrap it up so they could leave.

She continued to waltz from room to room and envision their life there, and ultimately Armando asked if he could use the bathroom. I told him sure, and pointed the way. After they left, I went into the bathroom and good old Armando had left some rather prominent skid marks in the toilet, which I was forced to clean up. Luckily, I caught it before the next guests came in. He was nice enough to run the exhaust fan.

TIP—Stock Up

Always make sure the bathroom is fully stocked with toilet paper, hand soap, air freshener, and towels.

In a similar story, about a month later I was showing a couple and their children around the house. I showed them the upstairs bath, which we had renovated with a brand new sparkling white toilet, Jacuzzi, and sink, and we began to descend the stairs back to the main level.

The (rather large) woman was bringing up the rear and asked to use the bathroom. I said to go ahead and we'd catch up with her downstairs. The tour went fine, and I went about my sunbathing until another couple showed up. As I finished up the downstairs part of the tour and began to ascend the stairs, I saw that the upstairs bathroom door was closed.

Chapter 6: Show and Sell 143

As I got closer, I could hear a fan running inside. Uh-oh. The couple were right behind me as I opened the door, and we were all greeted with a hot blast of rancid air that almost knocked us all back down the stairs.

The previous woman had not only "used the facilities" and neglected to flush, she had turned on the heated fan instead of the exhaust fan, and it had been running for about an hour. This woman had put good old Armando to shame. I tried to explain, but the couple looked at me with doubt, figuring I was trying to "cover my own tracks."

Always go back through for a complete check of the home after you give a tour. Another moral to arise out of these experiences is to make sure you have toilet paper, clean towels, and soap in the bathrooms. And air freshener. Had I not, who knows what else I would have found. After those experiences, I wouldn't be surprised if someone had used the shower curtain for unintended purposes, and to think of it, I'm surprised nobody ever took a shower while they were there. At least nobody did to my knowledge.

In the third related story, I was in our new apartment working at home one day, which was about an hour drive to the lake house. I got a hit on my security cameras, and took a look to see what was going on. I watched on the video as the Trailer Park Queen's large dog squatted on our nice, newly sodded front lawn, leaving a pile right next to our beautifully crafted for sale sign and brochure box. Sigh. The scene is immortalized on this book's cover.

I didn't want to engage the TPQ, who was still occasionally sending me hateful text messages, which I was ignoring. I was working, had a Realtor scheduled to come and show some clients in about an hour, and people frequently stopped to pick up brochures, so I couldn't just leave it there.

I reluctantly texted the TPQ to ask nicely if they could perhaps clean up after their dog, maybe have one of her kids take care of it. I had been paying her kids to cut my grass and do other odd jobs for me, since I had sold my mower.

I could have just gone to the police with the video of their unlawfully unrestrained dog doing its business on my property. She responded about what "keen sence" [SIC] her dog has, along with more poisonous vitriol instructing me not to place our directional sign on her property. There was a fork in the road approaching our street, and we found that folks were commonly taking the wrong way, leading them to the TPQ's trailer park, where the residents would glare from their front yards and windows.

We had put the sign up to save her residents stress, and keep our visitors going in the right direction. The TPQ told us to move it, or she was going to call the cops. So, we just altered the sign at the corner before that to include instructions to keep right at the next fork, and complied.

To keep our driveway clear for visitors, we usually parked our car in a common parking area in the cul-de-sac during open house days. This area, which was used by neighbors, was included in the road fee that the TPQ charged everyone each year. I believe we were the only ones who regularly paid on time. Since we had the nerve to ask her to clean up after her dog, she instructed us to not park there any longer, or she would, you guessed it, call the cops.

Things were getting pretty difficult on good old Crazy Court. We started to wonder if the street had gotten its name because of the TPQ, but again, to focus on selling our home and to be better people, we complied and ignored the troll. The moral here is to be ready for anything, and carefully inspect not only the home but the property as well, as often as possible. As the seller, it's not your duty to disclose information about bad neighbors, but if you are asked, you should be honest—your buyers will find out.

I guess there's a fourth related story. The most embarrassing thing that has ever happened to me, a long time ago, was when I was with a Realtor looking at homes. As we checked out the yard of one home, I must have stepped in some dog poop that had not been cleaned up. I didn't notice until I was back in the Realtor's expensive, brand new luxury sports car with white leather and carpet interior, and she asked "What's that smell?"

The situation was bad for everyone, and I was very angry at the homeowner. Even though I liked the house, I refused to go back as soon as I found a new Realtor after getting fired by that one. Talk about awkward situations!

How to Handle the Negatives

When we had first listed the home, we tried to think of its negative points as well as its positive ones. This is important to do, as your prospective buyers will certainly be thinking this way. Home sellers of course accentuate the positive, and fail to mention the negative.

Since almost of all of our appliances were new, and the home was well built, there wasn't a lot to worry about—except the furnace and central AC.

Both were the original units that were installed when the home was built. The central AC unit on the side of the house was rusted out and ugly. We had both inspected in the fall, and were told that they were functioning great, just on borrowed time.

We really didn't want someone to buy our home and then have the units fail on them. We wanted someone to be as happy in the home as we were and no drama after the sale. We also didn't want to replace a very expensive and functional HVAC system.

Our solution was to offer the home warranty, as I discussed earlier in the book. We were honest about the system with the folks who were interested in the home, and quickly added that it would be covered if it failed. Of course, we felt a high degree of concern, as replacing the system in the dead of winter or heat of summer could be disruptive, and home warranty companies have a bad reputation for finding ways to not pay for things.

When we lived in the home, we liked to keep the windows open to enjoy the lake breeze, as opposed to running the AC. We'd only turn it on if the temps rose above the mid-eighties Fahrenheit. After we moved out, I had to keep it set on a schedule to ensure it was always nice and cool. We were into another hot summer, and I wanted to show that the system was working well, in addition to providing comfort and relief from the heat outside for our guests.

At the worse point of a mid-August heat-wave, the system went out. I had installed a digital thermostat that allowed me to check and set the temp and schedules remotely with an app. Luckily I checked it prior to leaving for an appointment to show the house, and saw it was over ninety degrees inside!

I scrambled to the house and opened all of the windows, but it was still roasting when my visitors arrived, so of course they didn't stay long. Two HVAC techs confirmed the prognosis. The patient was DOA. My wife and I discussed the matter, and decided to put in a new system.

Rather than install a bottom-line unit as many folks would have done, we decided to go with a high-end, high efficiency unit for both the furnace and central AC, even though it was just the AC that went down. We knew the furnace wouldn't have been far behind.

We quickly assembled some bids and had a replacement installed the following week, and then removed the home warranty offer from all of our marketing materials. That set us back an additional

$7,000 that we hadn't counted on, and unfortunately came after we had dropped our price down to what was our absolute bottom. At that point we'd essentially locked ourselves into a loss on the home, but what can you do? Murphy's Law reigns supreme far too often. It did for us, anyway.

As our experiences have shown, you just never know what is going to happen next. Because you never know what your neighbors will say to visitors, the strategy of finding some way for them to have a stake in a positive outcome would be a good one, as we recommended in Chapter 5, "Marketing: Putting It Out There."

Our show and sell saga dragged out into early September. I wrote the preface to this book while sitting bored at the last open house on September 7th, 2015. Remember way back in April when we thought the house would sell in a few weeks? Always be prepared for the worst-case scenario. Always be in analysis mode.

We spent a lot of time trying to figure out why we hadn't received any offers. Conventional wisdom (there's that phrase again) says that if you don't get an offer after showing your home a dozen or so times, something is wrong. But we were well under value by every measurable means we could find, including over $100,000 under the Zillow estimate at its highest level. Even if the Zestimate is discounted as inaccurate we had the widest disparity of any home of our competitors.

I watched my list of competing homes regularly, and took some solace in the fact that none were selling. I reached out to the Realtors I knew, and heard the same things. The drought and corresponding low water level on the lake was hurting sales, real estate in NJ wasn't exactly considered a good investment, there was no true 'spring' weather that year (we seemed to go right from winter to summer) which is when people like to get out and look.

If the competing homes had been selling, I would have felt bad and looked at it more as a problem with our property, so we just kept the faith and forged ahead. Someone gave us a statue of St Joseph, which is supposed to be good for selling your home, but that didn't work very well either. I heard we were supposed to bury it upside-down, but that sounded blasphemous and the last thing we needed was to upset the big guy or gal upstairs. I probably would have ended up hitting it with the lawn mower anyway.

We actually did get an offer during this time, if you want to call it that. One day, I noticed that a neighbor's mom was visiting and they appeared to be enjoying the summer day with a few adult beverages outside. After I went home for the day, I received a phone call. A woman was shouting into the phone, and sounded quite intoxicated. It was the neighbor's mom, and she was offering us $375,000, which was really unthinkable. She insisted the house wasn't worth it, I'd never get a dime more and I should be eager to take her up on the offer. I thanked her but said no thanks, so that we could both go back to our drinking.

Summary

In the next chapter, we'll talk about what to do when that magical day comes when someone actually puts in an offer on your home, how to be ready for it and what to do when it happens. And you will finally see how our odyssey came to an end.

7 End Game: Closing the Deal

Renting to Own and Other Options

So here it was, September already. Back in April, when we decided to sell our beautiful lakefront home, we never dreamed we'd be in this situation. Remember when we thought it would be gone in a snap?

This was quite a quandary. The summer was gone. The Zillow estimate had been gradually coming down and down (perhaps tied somehow to the end of summer and this being waterfront). We had been bragging about selling so far below it, and now we no longer had that advantage.

We had always been told that conventional wisdom said that if you didn't sell by Labor Day, when people were trying to buy and get settled before school started, you were done for—might as well abort the mission, take it off the market, and wait until spring.

For sure the valuable boat traffic was gone, along with the passengers and their thoughts of how nice it would be to live on the lake. We had been in our apartment and paying the cost for both places for six months, and the emotional and financial stress was high.

My wife was talking about moving back in after our lease on the apartment was up. If you remember my description of what things were like for her, the car, and me back at the beginning of this book, it was a frightening idea. I wanted to be done with the house, the TPQ, the upkeep, the shoveling of snow, raking of leaves, cutting of grass, paying of things. I had spent the entire summer in my "second job" of being a Realtor and sitting in an empty house every weekend.

My tan was fading along with my spirits.

We had received several rent-to-own requests through the process, but dismissed them, as we were against renting the house by then, after our earlier experiences.

But then I started looking into it and discussed it with our attorney. It wasn't as simple as someone just renting it and then making a decision at some point to buy, although it can be done that way.

A true lease-to-own agreement has the renter make a deposit of 2-7 percent of the home value in earnest money along with the traditional security deposits. Then they pay a monthly premium on top of the normal rental rate, which is again held in escrow with the earnest money and put toward the purchase when they decide to buy. If the renter walks away, all of that goes to the homeowner/landlord. Since the renter is looking to buy the home, there can be a contract stipulation that they are responsible for any repairs.

We didn't know all of that, and it really sounded like a good deal for both parties. The renter gets to "try out" the house before committing to the purchase, and the seller gets to have their mortgage payments covered in the interim with rent income, and doesn't have to run over to make repairs. Those were our two big concerns, and this arrangement seemed to alleviate them.

We started taking those rental offers more seriously, but never did find one that worked out for us, because most of the folks that asked about renting to own didn't know all of that either. They wanted the simpler case, where they didn't have any skin in the game, and in that case we had no assurance that they were serious about buying the home later.

After the last open house on Labor Day, Monday September 7, I came home very upset and discouraged. I realized that after all of that optimism and expense, I had failed miserably. After all that time and effort, not one person had even put in a serious offer (discounting the gangster and the neighbor's drunken mom). I was burned out from spending every day working on new ideas, checking hits from the video cameras, chasing dead end leads, and planning our next moves.

I had a business trip that week to the west coast, and visited my son. He and his wife had bought a home when he was a US Marine and stationed in North Carolina between deployments. When he left the Marines and took another job that required relocation to California, they turned the property over to a management company to rent it out for them.

They couldn't sell it due to the many foreclosures in the area. They would have taken a pretty big loss, and were interested in keeping it for a while for the rental income. He told me some horror stories about tenants and the things they are capable of, just as my wife and I had feared back when we considered renting prior to listing our home.

He also told me about all of the great work the property management company did on their behalf. I got to thinking about how this would remedy most of the concerns that we had about renting, which were having to run over there to fix things, trying to collect rent, and vetting people properly before signing a lease agreement. We only had to pay the property management company and sit back and collect the dough. It sounded pretty good, but by now I had become much less of an optimist.

When I returned from my trip, I researched a few of the property management companies in the area and talked to a few through email and on the phone. I set up an appointment to meet with one the next Friday morning.

We had pretty much given up on selling the home, at least until the spring. A neighbor who was renting a house nearby had stopped by during one of our open houses and asked if he could rent with his girlfriend and her young daughter, as their landlord was moving back into their house.

They admitted they would be pressed to pay, as we required a lot more than what they were currently paying, but he could make some improvements that would help us sell it on the next go-round, such as a new upper and lower deck. I considered it, and had my meeting with the property management guy at the house that Friday morning.

> **TIP—Failure Strategies**
>
> *If the home doesn't sell, there are other options. In keeping with our theme of today's technology, consider listing it with AirBnB.com for rentals, or letting a property management company handle things.*

We were exasperated by now, and hadn't been able to enjoy much of the summer. The weather was supposed to be beautiful that weekend, so we decided to take that Friday off and go to the Jersey shore for a weekend getaway to lick our wounds and mull over our next steps. Rates are cheap after Labor Day!

Receiving and Handling Offers

After we had packed up the car and were on the way to the beach that Friday morning, my phone rang. I answered, but couldn't hear well due to the road noise. "What's that? Your client has a what? An offer on the house?" After all this time, I couldn't help but think I was hearing things wrong, or that someone was pulling a horrible prank on me. Was it the TPQ? It was truly the answer to our hopes and dreams, a Realtor whose client had been

Chapter 7: End Game: Closing the Deal

there and wanted to put in an offer. Yay! Hooray! That certainly improved the mood in the car. We were told we would receive the offer sheet via email later in the day.

Merrily we rolled along, turning up the music a little louder, rolling down the windows to smell the fresh air (not really, Garden State Parkway and all). The phone rang again. It was another Realtor, who said her clients had been at the house and it was one of their top two choices. They had put in an offer on the other one, and things had gone south. They now wanted to revisit our home later that day.

Wow, could it possibly be? We didn't want to be greedy. Sure enough, while we were at Martell's Tiki Bar sipping refreshing drinks by the sea, the second Realtor followed up and said her clients wanted to make an offer. So much for the 'conventional wisdom' about nobody buying a lake house after Labor Day!

It was hard to wrap our heads around the fact that we were getting two offers in one day. Could it possibly be that we might have a bidding war on our hands? We happily envisioned the two combatants bidding the price back up to what we were originally asking (it may have been the sangria that contributed to those visions).

At this stage of the game, the transactional stage, things can get a bit complicated. This is when the legalities come into the picture. Remember that this is a financial and legal transaction, so be sure to get every little thing in writing and conduct yourself in a calm and businesslike manner. It most certainly will be stressful, early and often.

The offer sheets and sales contracts are legal documents, and of course should always be reviewed by your attorney. I had studied up and thought I knew how to handle one offer, but having two offers was a very different and very fortunate scenario. We didn't want to blow it.

Since we were in vacation mode, we started thinking it would have been nice to have a Realtor handle this. We advised both of the buyers' Realtors that we had two offers coming in, that was about all we were comfortable doing on our own at that point. I googled some good stuff about how to handle bidding wars.

I emailed Jack Yao, the CEO of Realmart, the flat-fee company we had used, and told him what was happening. He told us about his extensive experience handling situations like this, and said that his team would take over handling everything from here for .5 percent of the sale price. That would include handling the bidding/negotiations as well as the rest of the details through the sale, as a normal listing Realtor would, but for a fraction of the usual 3 percent commission they would charge us. Extra services like this are a part of Realmart's business model, and it was perfect for us.

At this point, we were giddy and gladly signed up. We let our realty attorney know what was going on, and introduced them. Fortunately, I had brought the laptop on our mini-vacation.

When you receive an offer, the next important step to do immediately is to go to all of your websites and mark the house as "pending offer." This will shake out anyone that's been on the fence and watching the home. Could we even dare to envision a three-way? A feast of bidders after the long famine?

Later that afternoon, the first bid came in. We were disappointed to see that it was for only $380,000. By this time, we had the price listed at what we considered our lowest acceptable price, which was $415,000. This offer was low, especially after we had put in that furnace and central AC. That really put a damper on our spirits.

Vetting the Buyers

The initial offer is only a start, and where the negotiations begin. First of all, you have to properly qualify any offer. If it's from someone with a Realtor, it's likely that they have already been pre-qualified by a mortgage company for a loan in the price range they are looking, or the Realtor has ensured that they have cash on hand if they are going that route.

Realtors don't like to waste their time, so they check these things. You should ask to see these proofs, or they should be provided along with the offer sheet or sales contract. You never want to sign a sales contract or offer until you are sure about the buyer's viability.

If the buyer came to you without a Realtor, you need to ensure that they haven't signed a contract with a Realtor. Otherwise, you will have one angry Realtor who will be looking for someone to pay their commission, and it could turn into an ugly lawsuit against you or the buyer. If the Realtor had brought them to your home originally, whether you were there or not you are responsible for paying that commission if you listed on the MLS flat-fee or otherwise. You may want to ask your attorney to add a clause in the purchase contract stating that the buyers have not signed an agreement or introduced to the property by a Realtor.

Chapter 7: End Game: Closing the Deal

> **WARNING—Vet Every Offer**
>
> *Make sure each offer is legit, before you lose a lot of time going down the road. Ask for some evidence that the buyer is viable. If they came to you on their own, ask if they have signed a contract with a Realtor.*

If it's a private party putting in the offer, you can't be shy about asking. You have to protect yourself. If they are paying cash, you need to see some kind of account statement or proof that they have the money somewhere, in a liquid and accessible account.

If they aren't comfortable showing statements, they can have their bank officer provide a certified letter stating that the funds are in place and available for withdrawal for this purpose. You have to make sure everything is right through this process, or you will find yourself putting the home back on the market a month or more later, having lost all that time if things go wrong.

Remember, just because the buyers have good jobs or a lot of money won't guarantee they will get a mortgage. Mortgage approval is based on debt ratio, which is the ratio of their assets/income to their debt. Many of the people who are perceived as "rich" are really just up to their you-know-what in debt. It gets more complicated. There are different types of debt ratios, but that's up to the bank to deal with. You just need to have some level of solid assurance before moving forward at this point.

If buyers are paying cash, it's a very good situation because you won't have the normal hassles of waiting for mortgage approval and so forth. The larger the down-payment they agree to make, the more assured you should feel and the better the mortgage company will feel. Also, the length of time they have been in their jobs is an important factor. Typically one year is the benchmark.

The offer should also include a check with some kind of skin in the game to show that it's a serious offer. The check may be made out to their Realtor's brokerage company, who will hold it. If there is no Realtor involved, they should make it out to your real estate attorney's business name, because by law, it has to be kept in a trust account. This is the upfront or "earnest" money to show that they are serious about the offer. Around $1,000 is normal, but it could be more. Some Realtors use a rough guide of 1 percent of the offer. There may be a much larger deposit made a little later in the process, after attorney review, unless they have a loan such as a VA loan with no down payment. In some instances you get to keep the earnest money deposit if the buyers back out of the sale without a good reason.

Read the contract carefully, and then have your attorney read through it. Look for any objectionable terms or language, including the sections about what personal property comes with the house. We didn't want them taking my daddy's bull horns.

Make sure that you understand the difference between loan pre-qualification and pre-approval. Pre-qualification is a much looser qualification, and can be based on unverified things the buyers told the mortgage company, such as how much they make, how long they have been in their jobs, and how much they have in their accounts. It's pretty much based on the buyer's word on things related to credit and loan approval.

Pre-approval is much stronger, it states they are approved for the loan and have been fully and properly vetted by the loan company. Unless the buyer had been going through the process to buy another property, they probably won't have a pre-approval letter at this stage.

You should also find out what you are getting into in other areas. For example, do the buyers have to sell their own home first, and is that a stipulation in the contract they are presenting? That could take a long time (don't we know it!) Do they plan on putting down a reasonable amount of additional earnest money after the attorney review process is complete? Do they have that money on hand? Do they have a credit report that they can show you?

Responding and Negotiating

Of course, the buyer probably lowballed their offer, expecting you to counter it and then expecting to meet somewhere in the middle. So unless you are desperate, think before you blindly accept that initial offer.

When we were buying, Realtors had always told us to not present an offer that is a lot lower than the asking price. It's typical to offer around ten to twenty thousand less than the listing price, and that's kind of pushing it. Earlier, I advised you not do anything that makes the buyer think or know that you are anxious. This is why—if they believe that, they will lowball you.

Some buyers will make that determination based on how long your property has been on the market (usually with some coaxing from their Realtor). I guess our first buyers didn't get that memo—their offer was $35,000 less than our asking price, and just above the drunken woman's, and we had no reason to believe these new buyers had been drinking. All the while, we were thinking that we should have taken the gangster's $410,000 cash offer all those months ago. Who knew?

So come back with your response to the offer, or counter the offer by raising the price to one acceptable to you, and addressing any other issues. Keep in mind they may counter that again. Always have a list of negotiating points and concessions or "asks" that you can use in your toolkit. The price is just one part of the negotiation. Try to get something in return every time you make a concession. For example, you can ask the buyers to pay part or all of the real estate agent's commission.

Some options, such as paying part of the commission, may have advantages for the buyers. For example, they may be able to fold their cost into the mortgage instead of paying for them up front, which they may like if they have a good loan rate.

Any issues that are found in the home inspections can be negotiable as well—for example the cost of a minor repair. Physical items that may be left with the house, such as appliances, are also negotiable. If the buyers are anxious to move in, they may be incentivized if you offer to clear out sooner.

You won't get the chance to discuss a lot of those until the inspections are done, so keep them in mind. If you gave concessions during the price negotiation, use that to your advantage in these later negotiations by reminding them that you were flexible earlier.

In our fortunate situation, we had two buyers that wanted to put in offers. The first was an unfortunate low-ball. We finally received the second offer, which came in at $390,000. Wow, just above the other low-ball, but still a low-ball. I guess low-balling is the new thing, or it was just our luck again, but still a heck of a lot better than the situation we were in a week before.

Bidding Wars

The good thing was that now it was time to play the two buyers against each other and let the bidding begin. Jack Yao stepped in and at least got the winning bid up to $401,000, and out of low-ball territory. It was still disappointing to us to sell it for less than we had bought it for, and then do the math and see how much we were going to lose.

Signing the Purchase Contract

After the price dickering is done and you have agreed on a price and the details of the offer, it will be signed and accepted by all parties. It is now known as the fully executed contract. Again, make sure you are completely satisfied with that contract before you sign it. The timeframes for the next round of things that will happen should be spelled out in it.

Attorney review of the contract is typically done next in New Jersey, and takes about ten days. After that, there is usually another ten days stipulated to do the home inspections. In some states, the contract is sent to a title company rather than an attorney, and the inspection period starts immediately.

> **WARNING—Buyers in Control**
>
> *Despite the various deposits, the buyers really control the process and have a much easier time bailing out of the deal than sellers, (and keeping their deposits.) Protect yourself in the contract.*

Moving Through the Process to Closing

In our deal, after we had settled on an offer, accepted it, and signed the contract, things started to get a bit dicey.

The relationship between home buyers and sellers is like a dating relationship in many ways, but like in the old days of dating when there was a lot of interference from parents and other adults (played by the Realtors and attorneys in this analogy). When the buyers say they want to make an offer, it's a big love-fest. Then it goes through the other typical phases of a relationship, only in very fast-forward. Distrust, contempt, fear, loathing—you get the picture.

If everyone does what they are supposed to do, when they are supposed to do it, it's all fine and dandy. But when deposits are made late, deadlines for inspections and so forth aren't met, people start getting nervous, and the distrust starts to cause problems.

> **TIP—Stay in Touch**
>
> *If you get interest in the home after you designate it as 'offer pending', keep in contact with those parties in case your deal goes bad.*

Accepting Backup and Alternate Offers

During attorney review, you are permitted to take other (backup) offers. We actually did have a Realtor come in (yet another Realtor) who said his clients had seen the house and loved it and wanted to know if it was still available. I believe they may have been 'shaken out' by seeing the pending offer status change.

I told him that we were in review and they could make an offer, but to be fair we would give the present buyers the chance to match that offer. Another possible bidding war! However, his clients declined and said they would resume their search in the spring.

The process was certainly not boring for us; with new surprises every day. When attorney review was done, we could accept other offers in case something happened to kill the deal on either side, such as an inability to come to terms after the home inspection or on other aspects that were negotiated after the price was set and attorney review completed.

Or, there may be a clause in the contract that states that the buyer or seller can cancel at any time within a certain time period. More reason to read it very carefully, and have a very diligent attorney on your team. However, you can take backup contracts during attorney review, and hold them so that you are ready in case things don't go well and the deal is canceled.

The day after we concluded attorney review, we heard back from the Realtor whose clients were going to wait for spring. They had a change of mind, and wanted to know if the review was done. Unfortunately, it was. He told us to let him know immediately if anything went wrong with the deal. It was reassuring to have that potential back-pocket buyer.

Then, a few days after that, we heard from another couple whom we believe had just found out we had an offer. They said they had been following our home but had been too busy with work and travel to get over to see it. It seemed just perfect for them, and they had cash to pay.

We were starting to worry if someone was messing with us. This all seemed so coincidental and unlikely. My wife and I started to discuss who might play us in the movie version of this book. Certainly a comedy, so I opted for Clark Griswold, er, Will Ferrell.

They asked to visit, and I had them stop over the day I was getting my fire department inspection done. They loved the place and asked that I inform them immediately if something went wrong with the deal. Since we were locked in already, this was mildly upsetting for us, since both new parties were clearly willing to pay a higher price.

TIP—Keep Your End Up

Be aware of what your responsibilities are during the inspection phase. Some items are the responsibility of the seller.

Cash versus Mortgage and Approvals

In our case, the buyers started right out by saying they would pay cash "if they didn't get their mortgage." That set off some alarm bells and concern on our part. They showed a mortgage pre-approval with the offer, but since it was based on their "stated income," it wasn't worth more than the PDF it was printed on. When we weren't hearing much about how their mortgage approval was going, so when we asked about it they then said they were paying cash. We asked for some proof that the funds were available in an unencumbered account, and they refused.

This is something we should have made sure was in the contract, since they had said they might pay cash. Now we were more nervous, thinking maybe they were trying to hustle up the money. We had one or two backup buyers waiting in the wings, and we didn't want to lose them, so we were in constant contact, without giving too much detail about what was going on, and asking them to be patient.

Closing and Move-Out Dates

The closing date is another contentious issue. Obviously, if it's an all cash deal and the buyer doesn't have some kind of stipulation that they have to sell their own house first, you might get a quick closing, perhaps in just a couple of weeks, after the inspections have been completed. But normally it's more like a month to two months. Be careful about any requests for closings that are any further out than that. If they want to push it way out, find out the reasons. Remember, all that time will be lost if the deal falls through and you have to put your home back on the market.

You could hedge your bets by taking non-refundable deposits, if the buyer will do that. But if they are having issues or unsure, it's unlikely they will. If their intentions are good and they need the time due to some other circumstance, it's possible they'll agree to it. It might be a good way to feel them out as far as why it will take that long.

If you are still living in the house, of course you should be preparing to move out. In most cases, the buyers will want you out within two days to a week, if not on the date of the closing. This will have been negotiated in the purchase contract. You definitely don't want to move your things out until you have full payment in the bank and your mortgage paid off at closing. In some cases, it can be negotiated to stay longer and pay rent to the buyers until you can officially move. Be careful of the legalities and implicitly entering into a landlord-tenant relationship.

Closing Costs and Other Negotiations

Always be wary of the closing costs—they can be significant. There are traditional costs that are paid by the buyer and by the seller, but today everything seems to be negotiable, so be ready. In our case, we were selling at a pretty good loss, and we had at least one and maybe two backup buyers, so we weren't planning on conceding anything. Make sure that any concession you make is in very tight, crisp language that doesn't just say that you will pay for something, but how much maximum you will pay.

Remember, there are lots of concessions or contingencies that can be asked for at this point by either party. If you have had your home, fire, septic, pest or other inspections done within the last few years, the buyers may accept them rather than paying for new ones themselves. This can expedite the path to closing.

Managing Responsibilities

It is essential that you be aware of any responsibilities on your end. We weren't aware that it was our job, as sellers, to get the well inspection done, so we had to scramble to schedule it as soon as we discovered that.

The buyers will also have to have the house appraised by their lending company if they are getting a mortgage. If the appraiser says the house isn't worth what they are paying for it, you have a problem. Make sure to have a list of improvements and any other data to boost your argument at the ready for this inspection.

If you aren't using a transaction coordinator service or add-on service by a flat-fee Realtor as we were with Realmart, you will have to be the sheepherder and organizer throughout this process. It's possible that your attorney or title company may help, or the buyer's Realtor if they have one, but be prepared to guide your buyers through the process. Remember, the attorneys and Realtors have other clients to juggle. Check everything, keep everyone honest and the lines of communication open.

The best way to get anyone to do anything is to make it as easy as possible for them. Prepare a checklist with dates and follow up regularly to see if you can be of help, but don't follow up to the extent that you are being annoying or a pest. Your buyer may suspect you are rushing them.

Gary Marshall has good information on organizing the entire process, negotiating tips, and some great samples in his book *Home Selling Mastery*, which I mentioned in the Preface of this book. Sissy Lapin has a great website full of information, workbooks, DVDs and services to compliment her great book *Simple and Sold*, also mentioned in the Preface of this book. Links to both and other resources are in Appendix B of this book.

Always be careful with forms and legalities as the laws are different in every state. This book and our experiences are based on our specific experiences and how things work in the land of New Jersey, for example.

Be sure to keep your insurance company in the loop. Let them know the closing date when you have one. You will want that pro-rated check from them, and you don't want to pay for insurance on a home you no longer own.

Another surprise for us was when we learned that our homeowner's insurance was not valid on our home when it was vacant. You need to tell them if you are moving out. You may have to cancel your policy and switch to another company that covers vacant homes, or get a different type of policy or rider on your existing insurance. The logic is that vacant homes are much more likely to be broken into and vandalized, so some companies don't cover them.

Home Inspections

You may or may not be present during the home inspection. It's typical for the buyer and their Realtor to be present, so that the inspector can point things out to them. In our case, since we only had a remote/virtual Realtor, I was there to open the house for all of them. I stayed out of the way, working in my car, and came in toward the end to see if they had any questions. Make sure that the inspector has access to everything they need. You don't want a cranky inspector. I had refreshments on hand, made sure the house was a comfortable temperature, that all lights were on and access to all of the nooks and crannies where electrical panels and so forth were located was clear.

When the inspection is done, the inspector (who is hired and working for the buyer) will present the buyer with a report. They will then mull it over for a few days and decide if they will ask that certain things get fixed. This is another negotiating phase.

Our attorney was savvy enough to put a clause in the offer contract that stated that things that were simply "old" but still working are not considered negotiable material defects. We were concerned that they'd try to weasel a new roof out of us, since our roof was about fourteen years old, but still perfectly sound.

In our case, we continued to wait. We started to get nervous as we got out of attorney review and to the ten day limit and we had no word about the buyers putting down the rest of their deposit, and nothing about the home inspection results or scheduling an appraisal. We thought back and worried about their comments about paying cash if they "couldn't get the mortgage." Our attorney contacted their attorney and asked for proof that they had the funds in the bank as a backup. Silencio. The other private couple who liked the house continued to contact us, asking for status. It was a nerve-wracking time.

If your buyers do request that repairs are made, handle the situation delicately. Do the nit-picky things so that you can show you are working with them. For anything major, you can refuse, fix it, or offer them a credit to do it themselves. Perhaps if it's something that they are afraid will fail, but is still working, you can go back to the idea of giving them a credit for a home warranty, or taking one out yourself.

It's the same drill for the appraiser, if they are getting a mortgage. Make sure he/she has everything they need, put out the refreshments, have a detailed list of improvements that you made along with receipts if possible, and a summary of how you came up with your home price. The buyer should be researching and putting a homeowner's policy into effect, this is required for the closing so be sure to check on it and remind them.

At the same time, provide them with the information for all of the utilities and remind them to set up their service. Contact the utility companies yourself to let them know the closing

Chapter 7: End Game: Closing the Deal 181

date. They may require that you contact them before doing anything for the buyer, so do this as soon as you know your closing date.

A survey is also needed, and that's also the buyer's responsibility in NJ. Make sure you have your previous survey handy to give to the surveyor to make their job easier. You may even be able to use your survey rather than the buyer getting a new one. Check into your local regulations and laws about this.

When the title search, appraisal, and survey are all done, the mortgage company will begin the process of validating and underwriting the loan for the buyers.

The seller is responsible for the title search, which proves that you are the clear and legal owners of the home. This may also include a title policy, which is insurance for the buyer that nobody will show up later, claiming ownership, and that there are no liens on the property. If you have a mortgage on the property, the title company or escrow agent will be in touch to get that information so that they have the payoff info for closing. It's a beautiful thing to see that mortgage finally paid off.

You should get a copy of the closing statement, or HUD-1 statement, prior to the closing. Review that carefully. It will outline all of the charges that you and the buyer are responsible for, your mortgage payoff, and the bottom line amount that you will receive at closing.

You should see what you, as the seller, are responsible for paying for. This might include the buyer's title policy, property taxes up to the closing date, and the big one—any Realtor commissions. This is the part where you can be thankful there is not a huge sum in that space, i.e. what you would have had to pay if you had done the traditional 6 percent commission route to selling your home. At last, all of the hard work and insanity has paid off! The buyers have to pay for their inspections, appraisal, loan fees, homeowner's insurance, and property taxes.

Final Preparations for Closing

You will normally do a last walk-through with the buyer just before the closing, to make sure nothing bad has happened in the interim, and answer any last minute questions. We had to sweat through several bad storms, including an approaching category four hurricane, while waiting through this phase. It would have been a very bad time for us to have the roof blown off, but unsurprising, given everything else that had transpired.

While you do this walk through, be very helpful to the buyers. Point out where all of the user manuals and warranty info are for the various appliances, furnace, hot water heater, etc. Tell them about any little tricks in operating anything in the house. Make sure the home and property are still looking great, don't neglect that after you have a signed offer letter.

The last thing you might want to do before you lock up for the last time and bring the keys to closing, is to leave a nice letter for the buyers at the house with perhaps a bottle of wine or maybe a gift card to your favorite restaurant in the area. Make sure they have the essentials for their moving in day—toilet paper, paper towels, bottled water, hand soap, Band-Aids, a local phone directory, and any emergency numbers (it's no longer your problem if the home catches fire) In our case, we had our attorney represent us at closing, so we turned the keys over after the walk-through.

TIP—Better to Give

There has probably been a lot of stress through the process. Now that it's over, leave the buyers something nice before you lock up for the last time.

When you leave for closing, make sure you have your legal forms of identification (for both you and a co-owner if you have one), and provide plenty of time to get there. It always seems that obstacles present themselves when you need to get to a big event on time.

You will also need to let the closing officials know where you want your funds sent, if you haven't done that in advance. At the closing, do not be in a rush. Pay careful attention to everything that is said, and make sure to read everything that is placed in front of you to sign. It's good, not bad, to ask questions. It's easy to get into a trance, because it's kind of boring stuff, but stay focused right through the end. Fortunately, the buyers will be doing most of the signing. In fact, you may not even have to be present at the closing. Check with your attorney regarding the laws in your state.

When the closing is done, before you sing and rejoice about your mortgage being paid off, your home selling odyssey being over, and having a nice (hopefully) deposit to your bank account, now is the time to call and cancel your homeowner's insurance. Don't forget!

Summary

That's it. I'm done nagging you. Relax, smell the roses (one last time), and think about what you are going to do with all of that extra time now that you aren't playing Realtor part (or full) time. Congratulations! We'll wrap this book up with a few closing thoughts in the next chapter.

8 Goodbye, and Good Luck!

Wow, that was some story. Almost like a (bad) dream. What a long, strange trip it was, certainly for us, if you read through this entire book.

Would we sell a home that way again? Sure, because this time around we'd be so much smarter about it!

If we could rewind the clock back to January, knowing what we know now, what would we do? In terms of the renting decision, I think I would have looked at Airbnb more carefully. I still wonder if that might have been a better decision, but again for our own sanity we wanted to sell and close that chapter of our lives.

Zillow Talk has an analysis of what months are best to list a home, by geography. The bottom line is that you want to put your home up for sale when the weather is nice for home shoppers. We listed at the very beginning of April, however at that time the landscaping and vegetation on our property and surrounding it, the nice lake views, were all still dead due to another brutal winter. I wish we had waited a bit longer, until everything greened up. It didn't look nice for that first big swarm of visitors after we went live.

It seems clear that we initially listed our home too high. However I think we were doing the right things to price it back when we listed. Remember, I said that a home will always find and sell for its proper price. We checked the comps, the Zestimate (which we were well below), and did our due diligence.

Heck, the "expert" we trusted, the Realtor who specialized in sales on our lake, said to list it way higher than we originally did! We didn't know that it would be a bad "season" for selling homes on the lake, and there were external factors that influenced our ability to sell. I think that if we would have known what we know now, and made the other changes that I'm discussing in this "mea culpa" section, we would have gotten our original price on the property. If only I had this book when we started. Fire up the DeLorean, Doc Brown!

I think we should have replaced the aging HVAC system before listing the house. We knew it was ready to go, and despite our home warranty, it scared off a lot of our early interested buyers. People just don't want to invest that much in a

Chapter 8: Goodbye, and Good Luck! 189

home and then have to turn around and do a major repair. We should have put it in, and promoted it.

I wish we had known about the Realmart 2 percent rebate deal for buyers, and promoted that more aggressively. Many couples today shop on their own by going to open houses, then contact a Realtor when they are interested in a home, because they don't know how else to go about it. We should have had a one-pager titled "What to do Next" that outlined Realmart's rebate and services to the buyer.

We should also have signed up for Realmart's 1 percent seller-side transaction service. We ended up paying a half-percent to negotiate our bidding war anyway. It's really a good deal. They also offer attorney services for $495, which is a little more than half of what we paid.

Lastly, if we would have known the property would be on the market that long, it would have probably been better to have it staged, rather than showing it empty. Homes are usually on the market for months, so a three month minimum for furniture rental is probably feasible. We didn't price this out, so it's hard to say. Realmart is now moving into providing home staging services.

We learned and improved our technique as we went along. For example, adding things to our "buyer's kit" based on comments and questions from our visitors. If we had all of that right from the beginning, we would have done much better.

Essentially, if we had had all of the great information in this book before we had started, things would have turned out far better for us. Thus, I wrote this book to help others based on our experiences. That said, I truly believe that if we had not put in the effort we did, our home would still be unsold, like the vast majority of others who were (and still are, as of this writing) on the market. Or, we may have had to sell for much less than we eventually did.

It will be interesting to watch the real estate industry and MLS to see if they finally adapt. We stated earlier in this book that the Internet is the new MLS, and that certainly seems to be true.

I'm sure there are Realtors who are sure they could have sold the house faster and for more money. As time went by and our house wasn't selling, we were often asked why didn't we just give in and "get a Realtor." My answer was always the same—why? What will a Realtor do for us? We were already on the MLS. We had nice signs that actually had pictures and details about the house rather than advertisements for a Realtor and big photo of the agent. We had open houses every weekend, rather than rarely or never. We just didn't see any benefit, or how they could have helped more.

Did we spend a lot marketing our home? Absolutely. But nowhere near the $13,000 we would have spent on commission for a traditional listing agent. And we probably would have gotten a whole lot less for our money in terms of marketing effort and exposure. We could have had to do those things and pay for them ourselves anyway, because some Realtors we have seen certainly wouldn't.

So what ever became of us, after all we went through? As this book is finished up, we are enjoying life in a luxury apartment complex. We finished this saga just in time for football season, and I am enjoying my Sundays watching my beloved Green Bay Packers instead of sitting in an empty house all day.

We enjoy no longer having to shovel snow, rake leaves, fix broken stuff, and all of the expensive and unexpected things that came with owning and maintaining property.

When we were selling off all of our things, it was astounding to think of how much we had to spend on all it takes to own a home. Power washers, generators, lawn equipment, snow throwers, it's amazing how much everything costs, not to mention the time and money it takes to maintain a home.

When you factor in mortgages, insurances (mortgage, homeowners, umbrella, flood), property taxes, sudden catastrophic repairs like replacing the HVAC system, windows or roof, declining property values due to many factors, and everything else to worry about, is it really worth it? They don't call it the "money pit" for nothing! Buying and selling property is a long and stressful process on both ends. Life is short, and as you can imagine after reading about our trials and tribulations, we often asked ourselves "Who needs this stress?"

After seeing the radical changes in the real estate market in the past few decades, it's damn scary to invest that much into one thing. Aren't two of the fundamental principles of investing to have diversification and low administrative fees? Why do we ignore that when it comes to spending so much on a home that may not even appreciate, and will cost so much in "administrative fees?" The authors of *Zillow Talk* agree that it's a gamble, no longer the "sure thing" that it was in the past. If a stock you invest in goes bad, you can sell it and bail out in a minute. If things aren't working out at the blackjack table, you can get up and leave. Not so

Chapter 8: Goodbye, and Good Luck! 193

much with a house. You're stuck, and perhaps for a long time.

The American Dream used to be that real estate appreciation was a guaranteed investment. The idea was that you bought your place, made those mortgage payments regularly, lived in it until retirement, you later cash in big time by selling it for well over what you paid for it, and move into a smaller place, thereby funding your dream retirement lifestyle.

But lately, everyone I've talked to, including Realtors and home sellers, tells a different story. And ours is certainly demonstrative. Making a profit when you sell your house is no longer guaranteed. Rather than steady, the realty market has been all over the place. It's gambling now more than anything else.

With the economy being unpredictable, and the big lending companies controlling government officials and relaxed regulation letting them collude and conspire to provide home loans to people that they know would ultimately default on them, you now have to worry about foreclosures in the area killing home values.

Rather than the straight-line appreciation that was enjoyed for generations before us, home values are on the same roller-coaster that stocks are, although more graduated in the peaks and valleys. If you bought at the peak in 2006, you were pretty screwed after that for a long time and still, as of this writing for many due to the worst recession in the country's history and its aftermath.

Home sales are such a large transaction, and so complex, it seems that anyone involved has a bullseye painted on them by the sharks out there—including scammers and the financial industry. They are all people who are so much smarter in this area than the average homeowner *or* Realtor—and often with the government turning a blind eye to their abuse in the interest of improving the economy. How many families were hurt by adjustable-rate mortgages (ARMs), subprime loans, and other great "ideas?"

Many low and middle income families were "helped" into home ownership in the early to mid-2000's only to have their financial lives destroyed by the resulting meltdown when the housing bubble popped and drove us into recession. You are playing a high-stakes game against very smart people, who make the rules, and those are based on odds that weigh in their favor, not yours. These are bullseyes painted on the hearts of hard-working people who are just reaching for that American Dream.

We believe that this is why more and more people like us are seeing the light, and realizing that not only is it much less expensive to rent, but a very good thing for your quality of life, and makes financial planning and forecasting a whole lot easier. Too often, a home is now like any other asset that depreciates, like a car, and not a reliable investment. Homes in the lower or middle price spectrum are much more likely to depreciate than high-end homes.

Mortgages were designed for the way things were back in the old days, when you bought a home and lived there until you died. It's no coincidence that mortuary, mortician, and mortgage have the same prefix. A thirty year commitment was a no brainer back then, it was more the other part of the bargain (death) that was cause for concern.

But people don't stay put like they used to. We are an increasingly mobile society. To quote Carole King, "Doesn't anybody stay in one place anymore?" First-time homeowners, those young, ambitious newlywed couples who have always been encouraged to buy a home for the American Dream, may see a much better payoff by investing that money in their education, or a business venture.

We are a much more mobile, "agile" (to use an IT term) society. Employers aren't as helpful as they used to be in terms of relocation, either. With the escalation of climate change, you never know if the nice home you own near the water today will be part of tomorrow's lake or ocean. And that sweet mortgage interest deduction on your tax return? Very few actually get to take advantage of that, and it's primarily folks who are well off who do, if you look at the numbers. And there are ever-increasing rumbles to do away with it.

There is a section in *Zillow Talk* that talks about the break-even point in terms of renting versus buying, by geographic area in the US. They factor in many of the costs of buying, such as closing costs, taxes, etc. But it is an examination of the *financial* costs—not the emotional costs. Take a careful look at that, and whether you really want to deal with all that comes with a buying decision.

We now have a pool we don't have to lift a finger to maintain, a gym a few steps away that we don't have to pay exorbitant monthly fees to belong to (and we do work out more, now that it doesn't require a long drive in traffic), secure indoor parking, and if something doesn't work, we just make a phone call and go back to our television program. It's a beautiful thing!

Chapter 8: Goodbye, and Good Luck!

Our neighbors in this lovely community seem to have gotten the same memo. Many of them have kids of various ages and just don't want to deal with all of the above home ownership hassles. I think this kind of lifestyle is much more prevalent in other countries in the world. It works for us.

It's hard to describe the relief we have in our new lifestyle. If we don't like where we are, we can pick up and move somewhere else much more easily than if there is a home sale in the mix. No more paying property taxes and dealing with so many of the hassles. Another positive aspect of this was that it forced us to downsize. It's incredible how much junk one can accumulate in the attics and basements of our lives. We found we didn't need much of it at all any more. We took pictures of things with sentimental value we took pictures of and passed down to the kids or relatives who wanted them.

Our parting advice is to use your own common sense, as well as what you can learn from those who are experienced. Think outside the box, and be careful about "conventional wisdom." Old-school Realtors rely on it, but the world has changed radically. Conventional wisdom says to use a Realtor, list on MLS, you will only sell your waterfront in summer, don't have open houses on Saturdays or holiday weekends, and much more that we found to be untrue fallacies or outdated advice.

Be a rebel, fight the machine, dare to be different, take control. The world is different now, and so are your buyers—the new millennials that spend all of their time learning and doing things on electronic devices and who want things in an on-demand manner. They don't want to have to work through middlemen, they want control.

Did we scare you away from selling your home this way? We hope not. We did say it is a cautionary tale! Things probably wouldn't go as badly for you as it did for us, but in the end we are happy. We had some good years on the lake, and now it's someone else's time to enjoy the home. However, the process we used is not for everyone. Evaluate how much you want to do yourself, and whether it's even possible for you to invest the time and money it will take to go the route we did.

My wife and I went to the house the night before closing to make sure we had everything. I think it was a subconscious ruse. We moved from room to room in the darkened house, our former home, and reminisced. We held each other in the empty rooms, enjoyed some quiet moments, and talked about the good and bad times in our lakefront home.

Chapter 8: Goodbye, and Good Luck!

We assured each other about how happy we were that it was all over, but I think secretly there was a big part of each of us that wanted to undo it all—for it to suddenly be a warm summer evening and to go onto the deck off our upstairs bedroom and enjoy a glass of wine and talk about how we would get up early and spend the day in the sun, go out for a picnic on the boat, and maybe visit the tiki bar for some live music.

We left quietly, and said our silent goodbyes to the neighborhood and happily to the Trailer Park Queen as we drove down the road.

I had to go back the next morning for the walk-through before closing. It was a crisp and bright fall day. I stood out on the dock and the beautiful scenery across the lake greeted me. The fall leaves were brilliant in the sun, and seemed to be waving goodbye as the trees waved in the lake breeze.

As they did on most mornings, the ducks and swans from the nature preserve across the lake were feeding near our dock. As the ducks stuck their heads down into the water to find food, their hind ends raised up to me—a different kind of salute than the trees. Perhaps the TPQ had trained them? The ducks had always provided a comfort to me. Maybe I was more like Tony Soprano than I knew, and I wondered if Dr. Melfi had any available hours later in the day.

I felt a great sense of sadness, and yet a sense of freedom. I knew I would always miss the chaos of summer on the lake, and the quiet solitude of winter. I shut down the security system, and left the house alone and for the last time.

I went home after the walk-through and closed out the various accounts related to the house in our Quicken financial software. It was a beautiful sight to see the zero balance for the mortgage and escrow accounts, and to see our savings accounts somewhat restored. I called the homeowner's insurance policy and canceled our policy.

We now have an accurate view of our net worth, without the guesswork of what our home is really worth. It helps greatly in retirement and other planning. We suddenly found ourselves with no debt, which is an amazing feeling.

In the days that followed, I found myself feeling the old urges to check the security cameras, and thought at times I heard the familiar sound of the alert. It was like someone who has lost a limb having that false sense of feeling. I also found myself missing "the game" of playing Realtor. It was somewhat exciting and a nice distraction from my real job. We were one of the only lakefronts to sell in that entire time and I believe that is due to us outworking our competition, including the professional Realtors. I liked interacting with the enthusiastic prospective home buyers and their excitement about living on the lake. Huh, maybe I'll become a Realtor when I give up the IT business. Wouldn't that be ironic!

For now, we are recuperating and rebuilding our finances in our new comfortable space. We are planning ahead to retirement, and planning perhaps a new home purchase in those years to come—one that has wheels and will take us wherever we want to go on a whim.

I hope you learned a lot from this book, and that it saved you a lot of hassle and a ton of money.

Appendix A: Chronology

12/8/2014 Contacted our Realtor about renting the house out due to Lori's new job and the horrible commute.

1/9/2015 Signed rental contract with Realtor and began showing the house to prospective tenants.

1/10/2015 Began looking at apartments closer to Lori's work.

1/21/2015 Signed lease to move into new apartment on March 1.

1/25/2015 Prospective tenants visit house. First group is three dudes with a large bulldog, second is a nice couple who take lots of pictures.

2/2/2015 The nice couple request if they can rip out all of the carpets, put in hardwood floors, and paint the whole interior of the house white if they rent it out. They want the house and the boat. Looks like a done deal. Yay! That didn't take long at all. This is so easy!

2/5/2015 Turns out that the nice couple have incredibly bad credit, sketchy job situation, other issues. Deal is toast. Back to the drawing board.

204 Show and Sell: Selling Your Home Today

2/28/2015 Moved into the new apartment. Began listing homeowner possessions on Craigslist.

3/5/2015 Bail on the renting idea, begin making preparations to put the house up for sale. Downloading and reading books on selling on your own.

3/10/2015 Realtor advises putting the house up for $475,000 and she "feels good about it."

3/27/2015 Designed a nice yard sign on BuildASign and ordered it.

3/27/2015 Someone inquires about renting. They have two big Siberian Huskies. That's a no!

3/30/2015 Someone inquiries about renting. He has two big Boxer dogs, a wife and three kids. Another "no thanks" from us.

4/1/2015 Posted home for sale on Zillow.com. Listed at $459,000.

4/2/2015 Posted on Craigslist and Postlets, signed up with Realmart Realty and set up the MLS info.

4/3/2015 Began receiving email from Realtors offering to sell the house "twice as fast" as selling it ourselves. Dropped price to $449,000.

4/8/2015 MLS police demand that we take down photos that were from a previous listing of the house. "It has been reported. If you do not remove

Appendix A: Chronology   205

the photos within the 24 hours we will remove them for you." Sheesh. Drove to house to take new stop-gap photos and put them on MLS. Contacted several companies about staging or staged photos.

4/10/2015 Rental Realtor removed her lockbox after we canceled rental contract. Got new combination lockbox on Amazon and went to house to install it.

4/12/2015 First offer on the house, $410,000 cash. Too early, too low. We'd regret it later!

4/14/2015 Upgraded Realmart for $100 to get a page on Realtor.com for more pictures and descriptive text. Went on Fastsigns site and designed directional signs for open houses. Received staged photos from Virtually Staging and uploaded to MLS.

4/18/2015 Open House

4/19/2015 Open House

4/26/2015 Open House

5/3/2015 Open House

5/4/2015 Replaced front lawn with new sod.

5/6/2015 Dropped price to $439,000.

5/10/2015 Open House

5/17/2015 Open House

206 Show and Sell: Selling Your Home Today

5/31/2015 Open House

6/3/2015 Dropped price to $429,000.

6/6/2015 Disaster occured when Zillow overwrote all of our info with MLS info. Ugh.

6/7/2015 Open House

6/14/2015 Open House

6/27/2015 Open House

6/28/2015 Open House

7/1/2015 Dropped price to $419,000.

7/5/2015 Open House

7/11/2015 Open House

7/12/2015 Open House

7/25/2015 Open House

7/26/2015 Open House

7/20/2015 Furnace blower motor went out, no AC in the middle of a heat wave.

8/2/2015 Open House

8/9/2015 Open House

8/14/2015 Asked township for help with the eyesore lots across the street, further invoking the ire of the Trailer Park Queen.

8/16/2015 Open House

Appendix A: Chronology   207

8/19/2015 New furnace/AC installed. Dropped home warranty, advertise new HVAC system in all ads, and notify all previously interested parties that this is a new feature. Placed ad for vacation/investment home in the suburbs in NY Times.

8/23/2015 Open House

8/25/2015 Dropped price to $415.000.

8/30/2015 Open House

9/6/2015 Open House

9/7/2015 Open House

9/11/2015 Met with property management company about renting the house through them. Headed to the shore. Two offers on the house!

9/15/2015 Another Realtor said his client wanted the house. They didn't want to step on attorney review and would wait until spring to buy.

9/20/2015 Attorney review started.

9/25/2015 Attorney review completed.

9/28/2015 Private couple expressed interest in house, went over to see it themselves.

10/1/2015 Home inspection with buyer and their Realtor.

10/2/2015 Fire dept inspection for certificate of occupancy. Showed inside of home to private couple who visited on 9/28. They were ready to put in an offer if anything went wrong with our deal.

10/30/2015 Closed on the home.

Finis.

Appendix B: Resources

Simple and Sold System by Sissy Lappin.

Book: http://amzn.to/1OMmu2X

Book, workbook, DVDS:

http://amzn.to/1OMn9kW

Website: http://simpleandsold.com

Home Selling Mastery by Gary Marshall

http://amzn.to/1OauLuq

Zillow Talk: The New Rules of Real Estate

http://amzn.to/1PJicIg

Realmart Realty:

http://www.realmart.com/

888-362-6543 info@realmart.com

NY: 1745 Broadway, 17th Floor, New York, NY 10019

210 Show and Sell: Selling Your Home Today

NJ: 1110 Hamilton Blvd, Suite 2A, South Plainfield, NJ 07080

Virtual Staging Solutions:

(888) 201-9042

http://virtualstagingsolutions.com/

Build-A-Sign: http://www.buildasign.com/

Amazon lockbox: http://amzn.to/1OMnlkm or http://amzn.to/1OauV5d

Amazon brochure box:

http://amzn.to/1PJir6l or http://amzn.to/1PJiy1K

Acknowledgement

The author would like to thank Jack Yao, CEO of Realmart Realty, for his insight and help. There is no relationship other than the author as a satisfied customer.

http://www.realmart.com/

Thanks to our attorney Bill Mack, who put up with far more than he probably should have had to in closing our deal.

Thanks to Archangel Ink for doing a fantastic job of bringing my cover design to life.

http://archangelink.com/

Thanks to Trish Jackson of YouSelfPublish for the excellent job of editing my manuscript, and keen insights on the subject matter. I was lucky enough to find an editor who has also worked as a Realtor!

http://www.youselfpublish.com/

About the Author

Bill Hines has sold homes by himself, as well as through Realtors. He is an IT professional who currently resides in the Garden State of NJ with his wife Lori, their companion Khaleesi the Bishon Frise wonder dog, and one lone surviving goldfish.

Made in the USA
San Bernardino, CA
16 March 2016